BAPTISM IN THE
HOLY SPIRIT

International Catholic Charismatic Renewal Services
Doctrinal Commission

Baptism in the Holy Spirit
by the Doctrinal Commission of ICCRS

ICCRS
Palazzo San Calisto
00120 Vatican City
tel.: +39 06 6988-7126/27
fax: +39 06 6988-7230
e-mail: info@iccrs.org
web site: www.iccrs.org

Published in the United States by the National Service Committee of the Catholic Charismatic Renewal in the U.S. Inc.

To order more copies of this booklet please write to:
Catholic Charismatic Renewal
National Service Committee
Chariscenter USA
PO Box 628
Locust Grove, VA 22508
800-338-2445
Email: chariscenter@nsc-chariscenter.org

Cover:
"The outpouring of the Holy Spirit," acrylic on stretched canvas
by Veronica Dimae, Australia
Copyright © ICCRS

Cover design:
Jhorman Pérez, Venezuela
Stacy Innerst, Pittsburgh, Pennsylvania, USA

Contents

Foreword

It is with great joy that ICCRS is now able to present this book to the Catholic Charismatic Renewal and indeed to the whole Church. Like a good wine this text has been emerging and refining for a long time. It began as a response to the many requests that we were receiving at ICCRS from leaders all over the world. They were asking for a document that would provide some theological reflection on the meaning of baptism in the Spirit together with some pastoral guidelines for receiving and living this grace.

The initial work began in 2008, when under the direction of Bishop Joe Grech the ICCRS Doctrinal Commission began its first reflections. Gradually they put together a first draft text which was then sent to several charismatic theologians and leaders in the different parts of the world in order to gain further insights from a truly international perspective. Following this process revisions were made to the original draft and a revised text was produced. This formed the basis of the 2011 International Colloquium on Baptism in the Holy Spirit, which was held in Rome under the patronage of the Pontifical Council for the Laity. Sadly Bishop Joe Grech passed away in December 2010 but we knew that he would have wanted the project to continue, so with renewed courage and under the leadership of Dr Mary Healy the Colloquium went ahead. Around 150 invited leaders came together from 44 countries. It was a historic occasion involving many of the "elders" of the Catholic Charismatic Renewal reflecting together with younger leaders and theologians. There was also a need to listen carefully to each other and to respect the different cultural perspectives. Following the Colloquium a number of new revisions were made to the text and now we are pleased to share the fruits of our labors in this book. It is, however, worth noting that this important reflection on baptism in the Spirit, which is surely the heart of the Catholic Charismatic Renewal, is ongoing and in a sense is therefore still a work in progress.

On behalf of ICCRS I would like to thank all those who have had a part to play in the production of this book. We are especially grateful to the contributors and participants at the Colloquium and the numerous consulters worldwide. Special thanks go to Dr Mary Healy and Msgr Peter Hocken who are the backbone of the ICCRS Doctrinal Commission and the main authors of this text. I would also personally like to thank His Eminence Cardinal Stanislaw Rylko, President of the Pontifical Council for the Laity, for his continued support and guidance.

I am sure that this long-awaited text will prove to be a very helpful resource both to those within the Charismatic Renewal and to all those who seek to understand more fully the grace of the baptism in the Holy Spirit.

Mrs Michelle Moran
President of ICCRS
April, 2012

Introduction

On Pentecost Sunday, 2008, Pope Benedict XVI spoke these remarkable words:

> Today I would like to extend this invitation to everyone: Let us rediscover, dear brothers and sisters, the beauty of being baptized in the Holy Spirit; let us be aware again of our baptism and our confirmation, sources of grace that are always present. Let us ask the Virgin Mary to obtain a renewed Pentecost for the Church again today, a Pentecost that will spread in everyone the joy of living and witnessing to the Gospel.[1]

In the same address the Holy Father noted that the Acts of the Apostles presents the outpouring of the Holy Spirit at Pentecost as "the crowning moment of Jesus' whole mission" and the fulfillment of John the Baptist's prophecy: "He who comes after me... will baptize you in the Holy Spirit" (Matt 3:11). The pope then added:

> In effect, Jesus' whole mission was aimed at giving the Spirit of God to men and baptizing them in the "bath" of regeneration. This was realized through his glorification (cf. John 7:39), that is, through his death and resurrection: Then the Spirit of God was poured out in a

superabundant way, like a waterfall able to purify every heart, to extinguish the flames of evil and ignite the fire of divine love in the world.[2]

In these statements Pope Benedict provides the Church with a thoroughly biblical and christocentric understanding of baptism in the Spirit. From this starting point we can understand the grace of baptism in the Spirit as it has been experienced in the Catholic Charismatic Renewal.

The Catholic Charismatic Renewal is a movement in the Catholic Church that began shortly after the Second Vatican Council. Its origins are usually dated to a retreat weekend held by several faculty members and students from Duquesne University in Pittsburgh, Pennsylvania, USA, in February 1967. At the retreat the students sang the ancient hymn "Veni Creator Spiritus" and fervently prayed for God to deepen the grace of their baptism and confirmation. During the weekend many of the students experienced a powerful outpouring of the Spirit[3] together with the gift of tongues, prophecy, and other charisms. This "Pentecost experience" quickly spread to other college campuses and continued to spread across the world, so that today the Catholic Charismatic Renewal exists in over 238 countries, having touched over 120 million Catholics.[4]

The Duquesne event came about through the influence of other Christians who were baptized in the Spirit as well as the renewing impetus of Vatican Council II.[5] Baptism in the Holy Spirit had already been experienced within the Pentecostal movement for sixty years and within historic Protestant communions for seven to ten years.[6] The professors at the Duquesne weekend had previously been baptized in the Spirit through a small charismatic prayer group consisting of Christians of various denominations, and the students had prepared for the weekend by reading the Acts of the Apostles and a book by Pentecostal preacher David Wilkerson, *The Cross and the Switchblade*.

In retrospect it is possible to see God's providence mysteriously at work in the events of history, preparing for this new outpouring of the Spirit in the twentieth century. In 1897, at the prompting of Sister (now Blessed) Elena Guerra, foundress of the Oblate Sisters of the Holy Spirit, Pope Leo XIII wrote the encyclical *Divinum Illud Munus*, in which he called the Church to a renewed devotion to the Holy Spirit. The pope also asked Catholics to pray an annual novena to the Holy Spirit between the feasts of the Ascension and Pentecost, especially for the intention of Christian unity. On January 1, 1901, again at the prompting of Sister Elena, the pope invoked the Holy Spirit on the twentieth century by singing the hymn "Veni Creator Spiritus" in the name of the whole Church. On that very day, halfway around the world at the Bethel Bible School in Topeka, Kansas, USA, an outpouring of the Holy Spirit occurred that is generally accepted as the beginning of Pentecostalism. From there, revival meetings held at Azusa Street in Los Angeles in 1906, led by William J. Seymour, propelled the Pentecostal movement across all continents within two years.[7] Today it is estimated that over 500 million Christians worldwide have been baptized in the Holy Spirit.[8]

The Second Vatican Council (1962–1965) laid a doctrinal foundation that prepared in a more immediate way for the Catholic Charismatic Renewal. Of particular importance was the recognition in *Lumen Gentium* of the ongoing role of charisms in the life of the Church and the call to welcome them in a discerning manner. Also significant was the teaching of *Lumen Gentium* on the role of the laity in the Church, the teaching of *Dei Verbum* on making Scripture accessible to all the faithful, and the *Decree on Ecumenism* with its recognition of the presence and activity of the Holy Spirit in other Christian communions.

The origin and growth of the Catholic Charismatic Renewal have occurred at a time in history when the Church is facing unprecedented challenges due to rapid secularization. As Blessed Pope John Paul II noted, "Even in countries evangelized many centuries ago, the reality of a 'Christian society' which, amid all the frailties which have always marked human life, measured itself explicitly on Gospel values, is now gone."[9] Pope Benedict has warned that "In our days... in vast areas of the world the faith is in danger of dying out like a flame which no longer has fuel.... The real problem at this moment of our history is that God is disappearing from the human horizon, and, with the dimming of the light which comes from God, humanity is losing its bearings, with increasingly evident destructive effects."[10] The absence of God in contemporary society leaves a deep inner void, which people seek to fill with all kinds of spiritual counterfeits. There is a growing culture of narcissism, in which the highest values are placed on self-fulfillment, physical attractiveness, pleasure, and the accumulation of possessions. This in turn has contributed to the breakdown of the family and the assaults on human dignity that John Paul II described as the "culture of death."

In such a setting, there is all the more need for people to encounter the living God. Through baptism in the Spirit many have come to know God as a loving Father who acts in our lives in perceptible ways—who speaks, guides, protects, heals, and gives his children the fullness of life. This discovery brings an unshakable hope for both individuals and the Church in the face of widespread discouragement. God's sovereign action in our time has led to a new expectancy for the coming of the Lord and his kingdom. In all these ways and more, baptism in the Holy Spirit is answering the deepest needs of the Church in our day and preparing the Church for the future.

The purpose of the present document is to offer both theological reflections on the meaning of baptism in the Spirit and pastoral guidelines for the reception and living out of this grace among the faithful, both as individuals and in groups. Most of the content of this booklet is applicable to the whole Church, insofar as baptism in the Spirit is a grace for the whole body of Christ and not merely for the Charismatic Renewal. But the booklet is addressed primarily to leaders in the Renewal, since the need for such a document arose from questions that have arisen in various pastoral situations around the world.

Since baptism in the Spirit is a grace that renews the whole of Christian life, it touches on almost every aspect of Catholic spirituality and pastoral practice. This booklet will address only those aspects that are most directly relevant to the experience of the Charismatic Renewal worldwide and to the renewal of a "spirituality of Pentecost" in the Church today. The contents follow an order similar to the earlier

ICCRS document on *Guidelines on Prayers for Healing.*[11] Part I is devoted to a description of baptism in the Holy Spirit, its characteristics and accompanying graces. Part II presents the relevant biblical and patristic background. Part III offers a theological reflection. Finally, Part IV addresses pastoral issues raised by the experience and preaching of this work of the Holy Spirit.

Part I

The Characteristics and Fruits
of Baptism in the Spirit

Baptism in the Spirit is a life-transforming experience of the love of God the Father poured into one's heart by the Holy Spirit, received through a surrender to the lordship of Jesus Christ. It brings alive sacramental baptism and confirmation, deepens communion with God and with fellow Christians, enkindles evangelistic fervor and equips a person with charisms for service and mission. This work of God, which has been present since the beginning of the Church, cannot be limited to one current or movement. The present document, however, focuses on baptism in the Spirit as it has been manifested in the Catholic Charismatic Renewal. There are two reasons for this focus: first, the reality of baptism in the Spirit has been brought to the Church's attention in our time through the work of the Holy Spirit in the Renewal; second, baptism in the Spirit has been received and understood as the central grace at the heart of the Renewal. Through baptism in the Spirit the experience of the first Pentecost has been made present anew in our time. All the other fruits of the Renewal flow from baptism in the Spirit and in turn shed light on this foundational grace.

1. A Surprise of the Spirit

From the beginning of the charismatic renewal,[1] baptism in the Spirit has been experienced as a sovereign gift of God, not dependent on any human merit or activity.[2] The Catholic Charismatic Renewal too arose as an unexpected grace, a surprise of the Spirit, unplanned and without formulated goals and programs. The Renewal does not have any identifiable founder figure, although the many communities that arose within it do have founders or foundresses. The stories of the origins of the Renewal show that Catholics were baptized in the Spirit in many different contexts and in very diverse ways. Some were prayed for by others already baptized in the Spirit; some received this grace during their private prayer; some received it in groups studying and praying through the Scriptures, others through reading or hearing the testimonies of others.

Because it arose as an unexpected grace, the Charismatic Renewal does not have members in the way that organized movements and communities usually do. People are part of the Renewal first because they have been baptized in the Spirit, and subsequently because they affirm this grace and seek to be faithful to it within the Church. The organization of the movement was subsequent to its inception. The first structures formed within the Renewal were called "service committees" and did not claim any authority over the emerging groups and communities. Courses to prepare people to be baptized in the Spirit, such as Life in the Spirit Seminars, were devised subsequently to aid the fruitful reception of this grace.

2. The Characteristic Features of Baptism in the Spirit

The characteristics of baptism in the Spirit were well summed up by one of the participants in the 1967 Duquesne weekend:

> Our faith has come alive, our believing has become a kind of knowing. Suddenly, the world of the supernatural has become more real than the natural. In brief, Jesus Christ is a real person to us, a real person who is Our Lord and who is active in our lives. We read the New Testament as though it were literally true, now, every word, every line. Prayer and the sacraments have become truly our daily bread instead of practices which we recognize as 'good for us.' A love of Scripture, a love of the Church I never thought possible, a transformation of our relationships with others, a need and a power of witness beyond all expectation, have all become part of our lives. The initial experience of the baptism in the Spirit was not at all emotional, but life has become suffused with calm, confidence, joy and peace.... We sang the 'Veni Creator Spiritus' before each conference and meant it. We were not disappointed. We have also been showered with charismata. This also puts us in an ecumenical atmosphere at its best.[3]

This section will describe in more detail the characteristic features of baptism in the Spirit and its effects in the lives of the faithful. The ordering of this section does not reflect an order of importance or chronology of the effects. Some features are typically intrinsic to the experience of receiving baptism in the Holy Spirit, while others are fruits that often develop subsequently.

2.1 A New Awareness of the Reality and Presence of the Triune God

The most immediate effect of baptism in the Spirit is a new awareness of and communion with the Father, Son and Holy Spirit. In this sense baptism in the Spirit corresponds closely to what Blessed John Paul II often described as an encounter with the living Christ.[4] Jesus is experienced as the Savior and Lord who graciously acts in our lives today. The encounter with Jesus brings a profound awareness of the love of the Father poured into our hearts through the Holy Spirit (Rom 5:5). There is a new consciousness of the presence and power of the Spirit, through whom we know existentially that "Jesus is Lord" (1 Cor 12:3) and cry from our hearts, "Abba, Father" (Rom 8:15). The realities of Christian faith come alive. One who is baptized in the Spirit can say with John, "What we have heard, what we have seen with our eyes, we have looked upon and touched with our hands... this we proclaim also to you" (1 John 1:1–3).

2.2 Power for Sanctification

Baptism in the Spirit is a discovery of the Holy Spirit's power to lead us to deeper conversion and holiness of life. This is often manifested in a newfound authority to resist sinful tendencies, a freedom from addictions or deep-rooted patterns of sin, and the healing of relationships, especially in marriage and the family. The cross and resurrection of Christ come to be known as not only an event of the past but a present source of grace enabling us to die to sin and live for God. There is a newly awakened attentiveness to the promptings of the Holy Spirit, which leads to a deeper obedience to the Lord. Growth in holiness becomes less a matter of self-striving and more a yielding to the Holy Spirit. Where people respond to this grace in a consistent way, there is a lived experience of the Christian life as described in the New Testament, an ordered life of mutual love under the influence of the Holy Spirit (see Rom 12:1-21; Eph 4:1-3; Col 3:12-17), showing forth the fruit of the Spirit (Gal 5:22-23).

2.3 Praise and Worship

Baptism in the Spirit leads to revitalized worship, at the heart of which is proclaiming the praises of God, whether in song or in spoken words, often with uplifted hands. As people are filled with the love of the Father and a knowledge of the saving lordship of Jesus, they spontaneously respond in praise and worship. They are filled with joy as they join in the movement of praise and adoration that reaches its climax in the great doxology at the end of every Eucharistic Prayer: "Through him, and with him, and in him, to you, O God, almighty Father, in the unity of the Holy Spirit, is all honor and glory, for ever and ever." In this renewal of trinitarian worship the teaching of Vatican II on the Church and the liturgy takes on flesh in the life of the body of Christ.[5]

As the Holy Spirit hovered over creation at its origins, so the ever creative Spirit constantly gives rise to new patterns within the ancient tradition. Thus among the fruits of baptism in the Spirit are many signs of creativity in worship: a newfound ability to formulate God's praises in one's own language, among the less educated as well as the better educated; the widespread reception of the gift of tongues, primarily as a gift for prayer and praise; the phenomenon of corporate singing in the Spirit; and an explosion of new songs and melodies expressing the praise of God.[6]

2.4 Rediscovery of Prayer, Scripture, and the Sacraments

People baptized in the Spirit testify to a new thirst for prayer, Scripture, and the sacraments. From the earliest days of the Renewal people have come together in groups to pray under the leading of the Holy Spirit. Prayer becomes less a matter of routine and more a matter of the heart, a spontaneous response of love and gratitude to God and an expression of confidence in his gracious provision for all our needs. Many have found the Spirit leading them into contemplative prayer and the discipline of fasting.

The Scriptures come alive. People baptized in the Spirit discover, often for the first time, that Scripture is a living word in which God speaks to us personally and in which we find nourishment and guidance for our lives. There is a thirst for studying the word in order that it may change us. Texts that have been read before take on a new clarity, vividness, and relevance. For this reason the Renewal typically gives a prominent place to Bible studies and to strongly biblical preaching and teaching. Simple believers who are baptized in the Spirit sometimes show a profound grasp of the Scriptures and deep insight into the Christian mysteries.

There is a new awareness of Christ's presence and power in the liturgy of the Church, especially in the sacraments of the Eucharist and Reconciliation. People who were previously far from the Lord or received the sacraments only out of habit now experience them as wellsprings of life and desire to receive them regularly. The renewed worship that arises from this grace is seen most clearly in celebrations of the Eucharistic liturgy, the deepest corporate expression of worship of all those baptized into Christ.[7]

2.5 A New Love for the Church, Mary and the Saints

Those who are baptized in the Spirit find a deeper love not only for Jesus but also for his bride the Church. They perceive the Church as a supernatural reality animated by the Spirit and not as merely a human institution. Through close interaction with others they experience firsthand how the Holy Spirit brings unity in the body of Christ amid the diversity of gifts.

Often there is also a new closeness to Mary, mother of Christ and spouse of the Holy Spirit. Catholics recognize in her the first disciple to be filled with the Holy Spirit (Luke 1:35) and a model of faith, obedience, prayer, and docility to the Spirit. Just as she was at the heart of the praying body of disciples in the upper room, awaiting the outpouring of the Spirit (Acts 1:14), so today her presence and intercession are eagerly sought by those striving to respond wholeheartedly to the grace of God. Consequently, there is a new understanding and appreciation for her role as Mother of the Church.

Similarly, baptism in the Spirit often gives Catholics a deeper appreciation for the holiness and the teaching of the saints. They thus rediscover the spiritual riches of the great Christian Tradition of East and West and receive life and wisdom from the spiritual classics of the past.

2.6 Charisms

Baptism in the Spirit brings about the release of charisms, particularly the "spiritual gifts" listed by St. Paul in 1 Corinthians 12:8–10.[8] While these charisms have always been present in the Church, in the Charismatic Renewal they have appeared in a new abundance and at all levels, among clergy, religious, and lay people.[9] These charisms are understood as gifts not primarily for the recipient but for the upbuilding of the Church and the work of evangelization.

Wherever the Renewal is healthy and the exercise of the charisms is mature, the emphasis is not on the miraculous or extraordinary nature of these gifts but rather on their capacity to mediate God's love and build up the body of Christ. In particular, the gift of tongues has become quite common, and in this sense ordinary, primarily as a gift of prayer and praise.[10] In retrospect we can see God's wonderful providence in the teaching of Vatican II on charisms:

> Allotting his gifts according as he wills (cf. 1 Cor. 12:11), [the Holy Spirit] also distributes special graces among the faithful of every rank. By these gifts he makes them fit and ready to undertake various tasks and offices for the renewal and building up of the Church, as it is written, 'the manifestation of the Spirit is given to everyone for

profit' (1 Cor. 12:7). Whether these charisms be very remarkable or more simple and widely diffused, they are to be received with thanksgiving and consolation since they are fitting and useful for the needs of the Church.[11]

2.7 Healing and Deliverance

Through baptism in the Spirit charisms of healing have become widely diffused, and prayers for healing have become an ordinary part of the Christian life for many. From early on the Renewal embraced the ministry of healing as an integral part of its mission, recognizing that healing was integral to Jesus' ministry and that he empowered his followers to heal as well. The Renewal has given rise to various practices and ministries in which charisms of healing are exercised.[12] During prayer meetings it is common for people to pray for healing for one another; conferences and retreats often include time set aside for prayer for healing. Many have experienced healing of one kind or another, whether physical, emotional, psychological, or spiritual.

Healing is closely linked with deliverance from the influence of evil spirits.[13] Just as Jesus himself was led from the theophany of his baptism into the wilderness to be tempted by Satan, so those filled with the Holy Spirit also experience both the opposition of Satan and the power of the indwelling Spirit to repel temptation and to overcome the powers of evil. The age-old Christian experience of spiritual battle is lived anew, giving rise to a new awareness of the need for prayers and ministries of deliverance to free people from various forms of spiritual oppression.

The renewed attention to deliverance from evil comes at a time when formerly Christian societies, particularly in Europe, are experiencing new expressions of paganism that lead to forms of spiritual bondage from which the victims cannot be freed by psychological means alone. At the same time, in her missionary work among the nations the Church encounters the destructive power of spiritualist and occult practices, curses, and necromancy. As the Church is giving greater attention to the need for the ministry of exorcism, it is not coincidental that many of the priests who carry out this ministry come from the Charismatic Renewal. Here the grace of baptism in the Spirit meets a major spiritual need in the Church's ministry to the contemporary world.[14]

2.8 Mobilization of the Laity

The grace of baptism in the Spirit has impacted men and women of all states of life in the Church: the ordained (bishops, priests, and deacons), religious brothers and sisters, and lay people. There is no fundamental difference in the grace being given, as can be seen clearly in the distribution of charisms. This grace renews the lives and vocations of all the recipients—the ministry of the priest, the consecrated life of religious, and the service of lay people especially in their marriages and families.

While priests and religious have been active from the beginning, the Renewal has made a major contribution to the participation of the laity in the mission of the Church. Lay people baptized in the Spirit have been prominent in the work of evangelization. Many have been awakened to their call to serve in various ways, whether in the parish or in wider contexts. Many new communities have been founded and led by lay leaders. At the same time, the authentic work of the Holy Spirit always gives rise to respect for God-given authority and for the vocations and charisms of others. The widespread respect for Church authority that has characterized the Renewal has been one of the factors demonstrating the authenticity of this work of the Holy Spirit.[15]

2.9 Evangelization

Among the evident fruits of baptism in the Spirit is a zeal to evangelize, to proclaim the good news of salvation with apostolic boldness. People transformed by the Spirit become living witnesses able to speak of Christ from personal experience and from an existential understanding of the word of God. There is both a new desire to spread the gospel and a new clarity as to its content. The Renewal has given rise to many schools of evangelization and other programs in which people learn to share the gospel and exercise charisms as gifts given for the growth of the kingdom of God.[16]

In the first magisterial document on evangelization, *Evangelii Nuntiandi*, Pope Paul VI emphasized the role of the Holy Spirit: "It must be said that the Holy Spirit is the principal agent of evangelization: it is He who impels each individual to proclaim the Gospel, and it is He who in the depths of consciences causes the word of salvation to be accepted and understood."[17] At the very time that the encyclical gave rise to a much greater awareness of the importance of evangelization, new ecclesial movements were developing creative and dynamic practices of evangelization. The Charismatic Renewal has been prominent in this work, with charismatic communities pioneering new forms of proclaiming the good news, such as street evangelization and city-wide mission. The spiritual dynamism unleashed by baptism in the Holy Spirit is of particular importance in the context of Pope John Paul II's call for a new evangelization, reinforced by Benedict XVI's establishment of a Pontifical Council for the New Evangelization.

2.10 Commitment to Social Justice

Many in the Renewal have personally experienced the truth of the prophecy that Jesus applied to himself in the synagogue at Nazareth: "The Spirit of the Lord is upon me, because he has anointed me to bring good news to the poor. He has sent me to proclaim release to the captives and recovery of sight to the blind, to let the oppressed go free, to proclaim the year of the Lord's favor" (Luke 4:18). Receiving the Holy Spirit leads directly to solidarity with others and a special concern for the poor, just as in the early Church (see Acts 4:34–35). Many of the communities and prayer groups founded in the Charismatic Renewal have initiated vibrant programs of outreach to the poor, such as soup kitchens, homeless shelters, orphanages, medical clinics, rehabilitation programs for prisoners and drug addicts, homes for the disabled, and urban development projects. Many are involved in pro-life ministries or other activities that aim to bring about more just and loving conditions in society. In the Renewal such works of service usually combine a care for people's physical needs with a dynamic sharing of the good news of Christ.

2.11 Ecumenical Impetus

While the origins of the renewal in the Catholic Church show that it was not merely a consequence of ministry from other Christians, there nonetheless has been a significant influence from Pentecostals and Protestants who had already received this grace.[18] Baptism in the Spirit has thus had an inherently ecumenical impulse from the start. Catholics in the Renewal have experienced a new level of spiritual fellowship with other Christians who received this same grace, based on a common experience of deeper conversion to Christ, principally expressed in worship and prayer, leading to a love for the Holy Spirit's work for reconciliation and unity. These elements correspond to two emphases in the Council's *Decree on Ecumenism* and in the encyclical *Ut Unum Sint* of John Paul II.[19] As Cardinal Léon-Joseph Suenens wrote, "The Renewal is a grace for the Church of God in more ways than one, but it is a very special grace for ecumenism."[20]

2.12 New Communities

Just as in the early Church, so today baptism in the Spirit has produced an impetus for the formation of new communities in which this grace forms the foundation of a common lifestyle. These groups have become authentic schools of Christian life, holiness, and mission for Catholics in every part of the world. There is often an overcoming of barriers—personal, racial, social, denominational, or territorial—that had previously kept people apart. Community members experience deep bonds of fellowship with brothers and sisters with whom they share a common life in the Spirit.

There is a new recognition of our interdependence in the body of Christ, and our obligation to put our gifts at the service of others. Most of these communities are made up of both men and women, including married couples and families, and many also have members in consecrated life. The Renewal has also given rise to new religious congregations whose charisms are rooted in the grace of baptism in the Spirit. Many of the new communities, whether lay or religious, have become sources of systematic practical teaching and dynamic organizing centers for evangelization and other forms of participation in the mission of the Church. In 1990 the Catholic Fraternity of Charismatic Covenant Communities and Fellowships was inaugurated as a means of providing such communities with mutual support and a formal link to the hierarchy of the Catholic Church.

Part II
Biblical and Patristic Foundations

Baptism in the Spirit brings a sense of close affinity with the early Christians. From the beginning of the Catholic Charismatic Renewal, those who received this grace instinctively looked to the New Testament for the words to articulate what they had experienced. Although the noun phrase "baptism in the Spirit" does not appear in Scripture, it is adapted from the verbal phrase "baptize in the Holy Spirit" which occurs six times in Scripture. The promise that Jesus will "baptize you in the Holy Spirit" is one of the most frequently repeated prophecies in the New Testament, announced by John the Baptist in all four Gospels (Matt 3:11; Mark 1:8; Luke 3:16; John 1:33) and by Jesus himself in Acts 1:5, and recalled by Peter in Acts 11:16. Reflection on the contemporary experience of baptism in the Spirit should begin with Scripture, seeking to understand the full biblical context and meaning of the gift of the Spirit at Pentecost. The last section of this chapter will then look briefly at patristic references to this gift and its significance for Christian life.

1. The Old Testament Promises

Scripture reveals that God's Spirit was present and at work from the creation of the world (Gen 1:2), although it is not until the New Testament that the Spirit is revealed as a Person distinct from the Father and the Son.[1] Throughout biblical history, God made promises of blessing and salvation to his people. In the time of the prophets, these promises increasingly focused on the coming of a Messiah-King who would reign forever in peace and righteousness. A common theme in these promises was that the coming messianic kingdom would be marked by a bestowal of God's Spirit on his people in a new and personal way.

One of the most vivid images that the prophets used to describe the coming of the Spirit was that of water. Water, a necessity for life and valuable for every kind of cleansing, was an especially precious commodity in the biblical lands, where it is often in short supply. Beginning with Isaiah, the prophets speak about a time to come when the Lord would "pour out" his Spirit like water on thirsty ground (Isa 32:15).

> Fear not, O Jacob my servant...
>> For I will pour water on the thirsty land,
>>> and streams on the dry ground;
>> I will pour my Spirit upon your descendants,
>>> and my blessing on your offspring (Isa 44:2–3).

> I will not hide my face any more from them,
>> when I pour out my Spirit upon the house of Israel,
>> says the Lord GOD (Ezek 39:29).

Although God's people were spiritually dry and lifeless like a barren desert, God promised to bring forth abundant divine life in them, like flowers springing forth after the rain.

Ezekiel adds a new element to this imagery. He speaks of not only a "pouring" but also a "sprinkling":

> I will sprinkle clean water upon you, and you shall be clean from all your uncleannesses, and from all your idols I will cleanse you. A new heart I will give you, and a new spirit I will put within you; and I will take out of your flesh the heart of stone and give you a heart of flesh. And I will put my Spirit within you, and cause you to walk in my statutes and be careful to observe my ordinances (Ezek 36:25-27).

The idea of sprinkling brings to mind the cleansing rituals of the old covenant (Lev 4:6; Num 8:7), and suggests that through his Spirit God would bring about a deeper purification than is possible through external rituals—a cleansing of the heart. Zechariah expresses a similar idea, indicating that the Spirit will bring about deep repentance in the hearts of God's people:

> I will pour out on the house of David and the inhabitants of Jerusalem a Spirit of compassion and supplication, so that, when they look on him whom they have pierced, they shall mourn for him, as one mourns for an only child, and weep bitterly over him, as one weeps over a firstborn (Zech 12:10).

One of the most striking prophecies about the Spirit is that of Joel, quoted by Peter on the day of Pentecost:

> It shall come to pass afterward, that I will pour out my Spirit on all flesh; your sons and your daughters shall prophesy, your old men shall dream dreams, and your young men shall see visions. Even upon the menservants and maidservants in those days, I will pour out my Spirit (Joel 2:28–29).

This passage recalls an event during Israel's desert wanderings, when God bestowed the Spirit on seventy elders, who then prophesied (Num 11:24–29). Two men received the gift of prophecy even though they were not present at the official impartation of the Spirit. When Joshua complained, Moses replied, "Are you jealous for my sake? Would that all the LORD's people were prophets, that the LORD would put his Spirit upon them!" (Num 11:29). Joel's prophecy is an announcement that in the last days Moses' desire will be fulfilled. God's Spirit will bestow an abundance of prophetic gifts, given indiscriminately to all God's people—men and women, old and young, slave and free.

A theme common to nearly all these biblical texts is that the outpouring of the Spirit will bring a new knowledge of God. In Ezekiel God says, "I will put my Spirit within you...; then you shall know that I, the LORD, have spoken, and I have done it, says the LORD" (Ezek 37:14; see 39:28–29). And Joel's prophecy begins this way: "You shall know that I am in the midst of Israel, and that I, the LORD, am your God" (Joel 2:26–27). In biblical thought, to *know* is to have not just theoretical knowledge but personal, experiential contact; it is to be in relationship.[2] God promises that although his people have so often rebelled against him, his Spirit will finally provide them with the grace to truly know him and respond to him wholeheartedly.

These promises are the backdrop that helps explain the fulfillment proclaimed by the New Testament, already present in Jesus and his Church and awaiting its full consummation with the Lord's coming in glory and the renewal of all creation.

2. The New Testament Witness

In the Gospels John the Baptist announces the fulfillment of the Lord's promise to pour out his Spirit. John's message points both to his own time and to an ultimate fulfillment at the end of time. His ministry was in line with that of the Old Testament prophets, who pronounced severe judgment on a rebellious people but also their future restoration by God's mercy.

2.1 "He will baptize you in the Holy Spirit"

John declares that the "mightier one" to come, whose sandals he is not worthy to untie, will "baptize you with the Holy Spirit" (Mark 1:7-8). What does he mean by this statement? The word "baptize" was an ordinary Greek term, meaning simply to dip in water, immerse, or drench. In baptizing people with his baptism of repentance, John plunged them into the waters of the Jordan River, symbolizing the interior cleansing of repentance. It was not accidental that John used the waters of the Jordan to baptize. The Jordan was the river that the Israelites had crossed on dry land as they entered the promised land, led by Joshua (Josh 3). John was calling the Jews to renew their identity as God's people by passing through the water of repentance. He was at the same time pointing forward to a new Joshua, Jesus, who would lead them through water into the promised land of the kingdom.

By combining the ritual of baptizing with the biblical theme of the Spirit as water, John was communicating a powerful image of what Jesus would do. To "baptize with the Holy Spirit" is to immerse into the very life of God. John was saying, in effect, The baptism I give, drenching your bodies in water, is only a foreshadowing and preparation for the far greater baptism the Messiah will give you. He is going to inundate you with the Spirit of God; he is going to plunge you into his own divine life!

In two of the Gospel accounts, another phrase is added to John's announcement: "he will baptize you with the Holy Spirit *and fire*" (Matt 3:11; Luke 3:16). Fire is an image of purifying judgment (Ps 11:6; Isa 30:27, 33; Mal 4:1). Isaiah had prophesied that the Lord would wash away the filth of Jerusalem "by a spirit of judgment and by a spirit of burning" (Isa 4:4). The Holy Spirit's coming with fire would bring true conversion, a burning away of all the dross of sin, like the refining of gold or silver (cf. Mal 3:3). Such purification was to be a preparation for the final judgment at the end of time (Matt 3:12; Luke 3:17). Fire also recalls the burning bush in which God appeared to Moses (Exod 3), the symbol of God's awesome holiness and, at the same time, of his desire to draw near to his people.

Jesus came to be baptized by John at the beginning of his public ministry. The Lord submitted to John's "baptism of repentance" (Mark 1:4) not because he himself was a sinner

32

but because of his total solidarity with sinful humanity—a solidarity that ultimately would lead him to the cross. In response to this act of humility, as Jesus was praying the Holy Spirit descended on him in the form of a dove, anointing him for his messianic mission (Luke 3:21-22; Acts 10:38). The Spirit's descent upon Jesus foreshadows his descent upon the Church at Pentecost. The descent of the Spirit also recalls the creation story (Gen 1:2) and the dove that signaled a new beginning for the world after the flood (Gen 8:8-12). In Jesus and through the Spirit, God is bringing about a new creation.

The Gospels portray Jesus himself as the one "full of the Holy Spirit" (Luke 4:1), who carried out all his public ministry—his teaching, healings, exorcisms, and miracles—in the power of the Holy Spirit (Luke 4:18; Acts 10:38). He is able to "baptize in the Spirit" because he first received the Holy Spirit in his human nature.

The Gospel of John further draws out the meaning of John the Baptist's prophecy. Jesus explains to Nicodemus that the gift of the Spirit is linked with water baptism, which brings about a spiritual rebirth (John 3:5). Later, Jesus tells the Samaritan woman that the living water he gives, the Holy Spirit, will quench her deepest thirst and become a spring welling up within her to eternal life (John 4:13-14; cf. 4:23-24). On the feast of Tabernacles, Jesus stands in the temple and cries out, "If anyone is thirsty, let him come to me, and let whoever believes in me drink. As the scripture has said, 'Out of his heart shall flow rivers of living water.'"[3] The Gospel adds that "he said this about the Spirit, which those who believed in him were to receive; for as yet the Spirit had not been given, because Jesus was not yet glorified" (John 7:37-

39). The feast of Tabernacles was when the Jews commemorated the water that miraculously came forth from the rock that Moses struck (Exod 17:1-6). Jesus, then, is himself the life-giving rock (cf. 1 Cor 10:3-4), the source of the Holy Spirit, and we drink of that Spirit by believing in him. The passion narrative shows how the rock was struck: after Jesus died, "one of the soldiers pierced his side with a spear, and at once there came out blood and water" (John 19:34). From Jesus' wounded heart flows divine life, the Holy Spirit, who is given to us in the sacraments of baptism (signified by the water) and the Eucharist (signified by the blood). It is only through Jesus' glorification—his sacrificial death and resurrection—that the gift of the Spirit becomes possible (cf. John 16:7).

2.2 The Pentecost Event

In the Acts of the Apostles, the risen Jesus himself promises the baptism in the Holy Spirit. He tells his apostles, "wait for the promise of the Father, which... you heard from me, for John baptized with water, but before many days you shall be baptized with the Holy Spirit" (Acts 1:4-5). By calling the Holy Spirit the "promise of the Father" Jesus indicates that the Spirit's coming will be the definitive fulfillment of God's promises (cf. Ezek 36:27; Joel 2:28-29), the culmination of his messianic mission (Acts 2:33).

Jesus' command to "wait" shows that the coming of the Spirit is not under human control. God will pour out his Spirit when and how he wills. Yet Acts depicts the one hundred and twenty disciples gathered in the upper room as disposing themselves to receive the Spirit through their perseverance in prayer: "All these with one accord devoted themselves to prayer, together with the women and Mary the mother of Jesus, and with his brothers" (Acts 1:14).[4] The presence of Mary is significant, since she had already received the Holy Spirit at the Annunciation (Luke 1:35). The same Holy Spirit who brought forth Christ in the womb of Mary will now bring forth his presence in the world through the Church.

Jesus explains that the primary effect of the Spirit's coming will be to make the disciples his witnesses: "You shall receive power when the Holy Spirit has come upon you; and you shall be my witnesses in Jerusalem and in all Judea and Samaria and to the end of the earth" (Acts 1:8). Luke shows this prophecy being fulfilled step-by-step through the book of Acts as the Holy Spirit propels and guides the Church's mission.[5] The apostles ask Jesus when he will "restore the kingdom to Israel" (Acts 1:6), but Jesus gives them a new and deeper understanding of the kingdom: through their work of evangelization his kingship will be established in human hearts, in preparation for his visible and complete rule over the whole world when he returns in glory.

Acts 2 describes how Jesus' promise that they will be "baptized in the Holy Spirit" is fulfilled in the wondrous event of Pentecost. Pentecost was the Jewish feast that celebrated the giving of the law at Mount Sinai. But now it marks the giving of the *new* law in the Spirit (Rom 8:2), the law written on the heart (Jer 31:31-34; 2 Cor 3:4-6). As the disciples are gathered in prayer, the Holy Spirit descends in power. The dramatic signs of his coming—wind, fire, and a loud noise— evoke the theophany at Sinai (Exod 19:16-18).[6] The "tongues as of fire" that rest on each disciple recall John the Baptist's promise of a purifying fire (Matt 3:11). They are "filled with the Holy Spirit" (Acts 2:4). As Paul explains in Romans, this means that they are filled with the love of God: "God's love has been poured into our hearts through the Holy Spirit which has been given to us" (Rom 5:5).

The immediate result of the Spirit's coming is that the disciples begin to "speak in other tongues, as the Spirit gave them utterance" (Acts 2:4). What they speak about is "the mighty works of God" (2:11), that is, the great work of salvation that he has accomplished in Jesus the Messiah. Now they understand in a new way what Jesus has done through his death and resurrection, and they are able to proclaim it with boldness and conviction.

Pentecost is a reversal of the curse of Babel, when God confused people's languages because of their pride (Gen 11:1-9). The disintegration of human society caused by sin is now overcome by the uniting power of the Spirit, as people from scattered nations gather together around the Spirit-filled Church. Instead of trying to "make a name for themselves" as the people of Babel did (Gen 11:4), they "call on the name of the Lord" (Acts 2:21).

The gift of tongues is closely linked with praise of God (2:11; see 10:46). As a charismatic phenomenon it is a sign of the Spirit's presence, an invitation to faith. But it cannot compel faith: some people conclude that the disciples are drunk! (2:13). There is a hidden irony in the accusation that the disciples are "filled with new wine." In the Old Testament, new wine (or sweet wine) symbolized the joy and abundant blessings that God would give his people in the messianic age

(Joel 3:18; Amos 9:13-14; Zech 9:16-17). Jesus hinted that he himself would give the "new wine" of divine life (Mark 2:22; cf. John 2:10) which must be poured into new wineskins. Now it becomes clear what the new wine is: it is the Holy Spirit! Paul reaffirms this link when he tells the Ephesians, "Do not be drunk with wine but be filled with the Spirit" (Eph 5:18).

In response to the accusation regarding new wine, Peter stands up as leader of the apostles and delivers a speech in which he prophetically interprets the Spirit-event that has just occurred (2:14-39). The outpouring of the Spirit, he explains, is a fulfillment of Scripture, and especially of God's promise to distribute the gift of prophecy among all his people (Joel 2:28-32). The gift of the Spirit makes the Church a community of prophets, that is, men and women who are able to speak God's word and interpret God's mighty deeds under the influence of the Holy Spirit. Prophecy can include visions and dreams (2:17), which are frequent in Acts.[7] These charisms are a sign that the "last days" have begun, although the Spirit's work will be completed only on the "day of the Lord" (2:20), the day of Jesus' coming in glory and the resurrection of the dead.

In his summary of the good news (2:22-36), Peter explains that the gift of the Spirit is a direct consequence of the resurrection and ascension of Jesus: "Being therefore exalted at the right hand of God, and having received from the Father the promise of the Holy Spirit, he has poured out this which you see and hear." Because Jesus himself received the Spirit in his glorified humanity, he can pour out the Spirit on his Church (cf. John 7:39)—a gift that is already experienced now but will reach final fulfillment in the resurrection on the last day (Acts 24:15).

Luke depicts the result of anointed preaching in the Spirit: at the conclusion of Peter's speech the listeners are "cut to the heart," that is, they experience deep conviction of sin and an awareness of their need for forgiveness. When they ask Peter what to do, he responds, "repent and be baptized... and you shall receive the gift of the Holy Spirit" (2:38).

The Effects of Baptism in the Spirit

Throughout Acts it is evident that the coming of the Spirit is not something imperceptible but a visible, unmistakable reality, "what you see and hear" (Acts 2:33).[8] Those who receive the Spirit are immediately aware of his presence and activity in their lives. The effects of baptism in the Holy Spirit as portrayed in Acts can be summed up as follows.

The Spirit brings a transformation of life. This is especially evident in Peter: the doubting, fearful fisherman who had denied Jesus three times is hardly recognizable in the bold, Spirit-filled Peter who preaches to thousands and heals a crippled man by a word. The Spirit creates an atmosphere of joy and continual praise, even in the face of persecution.[9] The charisms of prophecy and of tongues, closely linked with praise of God, are especially evident.[10] The disciples do many signs and wonders in the name of Jesus. There is a new boldness to proclaim the good news, even at the risk of beatings, imprisonment, and martyrdom.[11] Finally, the Pentecost event gives the early Christians a deep communion with one another, a unity of heart that goes far beyond the limits of common interests, compatible personalities, or shared socio-economic background (Acts 2:42; 4:32).

Baptism, the Laying on of Hands, and the Gift of the Spirit

Although Pentecost is a unique, paradigmatic event for the Church, it is also a grace that is continually renewed and deepened. The response of Peter in Acts 2:38 affirms the relationship between the Pentecost experience and sacramental baptism. Peter indicates that the gift of the Spirit is mediated through the Church by means of baptism in water. Thus there is a profound inner connection between the sacrament and the Pentecost experience. Although this is the norm, Luke also reports occasions when baptism and the outpouring of the Spirit do not occur simultaneously.

In the account of the "Samaritan Pentecost," Philip baptizes some Samaritans who believe the gospel through his preaching. But they receive the Spirit only after the apostles come from Jerusalem and lay hands on them (Acts 8:12-17; cf. 9:17-18; 19:5-6)[12]—a gesture that the Church recognizes as part of the origin of the sacrament of confirmation.[13] The opposite order occurs in the "Gentile Pentecost" (Acts 10-11), where Cornelius and his household are baptized in the Spirit prior to any sacramental rite. Luke indicates that the reason for this is that the first baptism of gentiles was a major milestone in the development of the Church. That even gentiles could be included among God's people was such a radically new idea that God had to make it unmistakably clear. Luke depicts how the Holy Spirit orchestrates the whole event: Cornelius is visited by an angel, Peter receives a heavenly vision, the Spirit speaks directly to Peter, and a delegation from Cornelius arrives at just that moment. The culmination of the story comes as Peter is preaching the gospel to Cornelius and his assembled friends:

> While Peter was still speaking, the Holy Spirit fell on all who heard the word. And the believers from among the circumcised who came with Peter were amazed, because the gift of the Holy Spirit had been poured out even on the gentiles. For they heard them speaking in tongues and extolling God. Then Peter declared, "Can any one forbid water for baptizing these people who have received the Holy Spirit just as we have?" And he commanded them to be baptized in the name of Jesus Christ (Acts 10:44–48).

The descent of the Spirit in a perceptible way, as on the day of Pentecost, serves as an irrefutable sign that God is offering the gift of salvation to these gentiles. When Peter later recounts the incident, his hearers exclaim with amazement, "Then to the gentiles also God has granted repentance unto life!" (Acts 11:18).

Luke also notes another occasion when the Pentecost experience is repeated. In Acts 4, as the Church begins to undergo persecution, the disciples pray not for protection but for greater boldness in preaching the word and for signs and wonders to accompany the message. In response to their prayer, "The place in which they were gathered together was shaken; and they were all filled with the Holy Spirit and spoke the word of God with boldness" (Acts 4:31).

These varied episodes indicate that God is not limited in how he can impart the Spirit. To become a Christian means to be baptized in the name of Jesus Christ and to receive the perceptible outpouring of the Holy Spirit. These are normally a single reality, but due to various circumstances one can occur without the other. In such a case, what is missing, either sacramental baptism or the Pentecost experience, needs to be supplied.

Baptism in the Spirit and the Church's Mission

The Acts of the Apostles could well be called the Acts of the Holy Spirit, because the Spirit appears everywhere and directs all the activity of the Church (Acts 1:6-11). Every new step in the Church's mission is led by the Holy Spirit, including the baptism of gentiles (Acts 8:26-39; 10:1-48), the missionary journey of Paul and Barnabas (13:1-3), and the extension of the mission into Europe (16:9-10). The Spirit sometimes explicitly tells an evangelist what to do (8:29) or prevents disciples from going where they had planned (16:6-7). Being directly led by the Spirit is, like prophecy, part of the ordinary functioning of the Church.

At the same time Acts makes clear that the highest office in the Church, and the primary channel for the Spirit's working, is that of the apostles. Jesus gave instructions through the Holy Spirit to the apostles (Acts 1:2), and it is they who discern and oversee each new step taken by the Church under the leading of the Spirit (8:14; 11:22; 15:2, 6). At the council of Jerusalem, concerning the inclusion of the gentiles, the apostles indicate that their authoritative decision was guided by the Holy Spirit: "it seemed good to the Holy Spirit and to us" (15:28). There is no contradiction between the Spirit's spontaneous leading and the apostles' responsibility to supervise and order the life of the Church. Both are gifts of the Spirit.

2.3 St. Paul and the Gift of the Spirit

The letters of Paul are filled with references to the Holy Spirit's activity in the Church and the life of the believer. Although Paul does not use the term "baptize in the Holy Spirit," he is clearly familiar with the kind of Spirit-experience described in Acts. His letters, written earlier than the Gospels and Acts, display an intense concern for fostering and properly pastoring the work of the Spirit in the local church. Whereas Luke shows the presence and power of the Holy Spirit primarily through the Church's visible activity, especially her missionary activity, Paul reveals more about the Spirit's interior sanctifying work.

Receiving the Spirit

For Paul, as for Luke, receiving the Spirit is a perceptible event that takes place through anointed preaching of the gospel and its acceptance in faith. Paul often reminds his readers of this conversion event, taking for granted that they are keenly aware of having experienced the gift of the Spirit. He reminds the Thessalonians that "our gospel came to you not only in word, but also in power (*dynamis*) and in the Holy Spirit and with full conviction" (1 Thes 1:5). Similarly, his preaching in Corinth was "not in plausible words of wisdom, but in demonstration of Spirit and of power (*dynamis*)" (1 Cor 2:4). The "power" probably refers both to charismatic activity (miracles, tongues, and prophecy) and to the inner experience of being convinced beyond any doubt of the truth of the gospel.[14] Paul's appeal to the Galatians again presupposes such perceptible experience: "Did you receive the Spirit by works of the law, or by hearing with faith? ... Did you experience so many things in vain? ... Does he who supplies the Spirit to you and works miracles (*dynameis*) among you do so by works of the law, or by hearing with faith?" (Gal 3:2–5). The Spirit's presence in a believer's heart is so perceptible that Paul can call it a "pledge" or "guarantee" of our glorious inheritance in the life to come (2 Cor 1:22; 5:5; Eph 1:13; see Rom 8:23). Receiving the Spirit serves as both a powerful confirmation of the truth of the apostolic preaching and a foundation for further spiritual growth.

In several passages Paul closely links receiving the Spirit with baptism. To be baptized is to be "washed" in the Spirit (1 Cor 6:11) and to "drink of the one Spirit" (1 Cor 12:13). Baptism is a "renewal in the Holy Spirit" (Titus 3:5), but it is also the beginning of a lifelong process in which the believer is renewed day by day (2 Cor 4:16; cf. Rom 12:2; Eph 4:23–24).

Life in the Spirit

The powerful Spirit experience to which Paul appeals is not a vague religious experience or a "spiritual high." It is experience *of the reality of the gospel*—of God's love manifested in the death and resurrection of his Son Jesus, freeing us from sin and bringing us into a new relationship with himself (Rom 5:5; Eph 1:5–8). The Holy Spirit makes Christ's work of redemption an efficacious reality, an energy that gradually permeates the believer's whole life. Paul describes this ongoing work of the Spirit in a variety of ways: revelation, sanctification, freedom, renewal, sonship.

The Spirit operates principally within the heart, the hidden center of the person. The Spirit enlightens the eyes of the heart (cf. Eph 1:18) by revealing the gifts of God, "what God has prepared for those who love him" (1 Cor 2:9-12). That is, the Spirit makes known in a personal way the gift God has given in sending us his Son. Through the Spirit, God reveals not merely doctrines or precepts but *himself* (1 Cor 2:11). Christians come to know Jesus as Savior by *being saved*, and come to know God as "Abba, Father" by *becoming* his son or daughter (Rom 8:15; Gal 4:6).

The Holy Spirit's revelation leads to a progressive transformation of life: "And we all, with unveiled face, beholding the glory of the Lord, are being changed into his likeness from glory to glory; for this comes from the Lord who is the Spirit" (2 Cor 3:18; cf. Rom 8:29; Col 3:10). Paul often describes this process as sanctification, that is, becoming holy, "set apart" for God. Christians are already sanctified through the Spirit in baptism (1 Cor 1:2; 6:11), yet are being sanctified as they cooperate with the ongoing work of the Spirit (Rom 15:16; 1 Thes 4:3; 5:23).

The Spirit brings freedom from the law (Rom 8:2; Gal 5:18), that is the law experienced as an external constraint that threatens us with condemnation (Rom 8:1; Gal 3:10). Instead, the Spirit moves us to yield to God spontaneously from within the heart, to respond to him with filial love, trust, and obedience. Thus the Christian life is described as "walking by the Spirit" (Gal 5:16, 25) or being "led by the Spirit" (Rom 8:14; Gal 5:18).

Although sanctification is God's work, not a human work, the believer is by no means passive in this process. To receive the Spirit is to begin an ongoing battle: the war between flesh and spirit, between the human inclination toward sin and the Spirit's promptings toward holiness. It is a lifelong battle, in which one must constantly choose to yield to the Spirit and reject the flesh. Paul exhorts, "Walk by the Spirit, and do not gratify the desires of the flesh. For the desires of the flesh are against the Spirit, and the desires of the Spirit are against the flesh" (Gal 5:16-17; see Rom 8:1-13). The Spirit's sanctifying work in a person will be complete only at the resurrection from the dead, when the body itself will be become a "spiritual body" and share in divine glory (1 Cor 15:44-49).

The Charisms of the Spirit

Paul's teaching on life in the Spirit is the necessary context for understanding the charisms of the Spirit. A charism, also called a "gift" (Eph 4:7-8) or "working" or "manifestation" (1 Cor 12:6-7) of the Spirit, is a gift freely bestowed by the Spirit for building up the body of Christ. Charisms are not merely natural endowments or acquired skills. They are supernatural gifts that either enable what is humanly impossible (such as healings or miracles) or enhance a natural gift, such as teaching or service, to a level of supernatural efficacy. Paul's most extensive teaching on charisms is in 1 Cor 12-14, within a larger section on proper conduct in the liturgy (1 Cor 11-14).

Paul emphasizes that charisms are freely distributed by the Holy Spirit as he wills. Charisms are distinct from the sanctifying grace given at baptism, in that they are given not primarily for the personal sanctification of the recipient but to be exercised for the good of others. The charisms are forms of "service" (1 Cor 12:5) because their purpose is to serve others. The marvelous diversity of charisms is ordered to the Church's unity, founded on the unity of the one God—Father, Son, and Holy Spirit (12:4-6).

Charisms are given to *every* member of the body of Christ for the common good (1 Cor 12:7; Eph 4:7). All play a part in building up the Church and advancing her mission. All have a responsibility to exercise the gifts they have been given: "Since we have gifts that differ according to the grace given to us, let us exercise them" (Rom 12:6; cf. 1 Pet 4:10). Although the gifts are given freely, Christians are to "strive eagerly" for them because of their powerful capacity to edify others (1 Cor 12:31; 14:1).

Paul warns the Corinthians that charisms are not in themselves a measure of holiness (cf. Acts 3:12; 1 Cor 13:1-3). Even in their pagan past they experienced some seemingly charismatic phenomena (1 Cor 12:2). Jesus had warned that many will say to him, "Lord, Lord, did we not prophesy in your name, and cast out demons in your name, and do many mighty works in your name?" to whom he will declare, "I never knew you; depart from me, you evildoers" (Matt 7:22-23). These texts indicate that it is possible for people to exercise charisms while teaching or living in ways that are incompatible with Christian faith. On the other hand, growth in holiness normally leads to a greater fruitfulness in the exercise of charisms. Charisms must be discerned, and the basic criteria are that they acknowledge the lordship of Jesus and authentically serve the mission of his Church (1 Cor 12:3; 14:7–26).

At the center of Paul's teaching on charisms is his great hymn to love (*agape*) in 1 Cor 13. This chapter is not a digression but rather provides the foundational principle that must order all the exercise of charisms. Even the greatest charisms are nothing apart from love (13:1–3). Whereas charisms will one day pass away, faith, hope, and love will last (13:8–13).[15] Paul does not speak of love itself as a charism but as a "way" (*hodos*), the path along which charisms must be exercised, the motive and measure for their use (1 Cor 12:31). After explaining this principle in chapter 13, Paul applies it to the use of charisms in chapter 14, where he warns the Corinthians against an immature, self-serving use of charisms. The purpose of the gifts is not to stir up excitement or draw attention to oneself, nor even, with the exception of tongues as a personal prayer language, to build up oneself (1 Cor 14:4). Rather, the gifts are primarily for building up others in love. Paul is not setting up an opposition between charisms and love, but rather between charisms exercised with or without love. Indeed, his whole point is that *exercising a charism must itself be an act of love.*

Paul's letters contain several lists of charisms, none of which is meant to be systematic or complete. The most extensive is in 1 Cor 12:8–10 (cf. 12:28–30), which lists word of wisdom, word of knowledge, faith, healings, working of miracles, prophecy, discernment of spirits, tongues, and interpretation of tongues. Paul refers to these as "spiritual gifts" (*pneumatika*, 12:1; 14:1), perhaps because they are especially dependent on docility to the Spirit. The "word of wisdom" and "word of knowledge" probably refer to Spirit-inspired utterances that give new insight into God's plan of salvation and its practical application in the life of believers. A "word of knowledge" may also refer to supernatural knowledge of certain facts, such as Jesus' knowledge of the Samaritan woman's past (John 4:17) or Ananias's knowledge of the conversion of Saul (Acts 9:10-12). "Faith" here is not the justifying faith common to all believers, but a confident assurance that God is about to act in a particular situation, the kind of faith that Jesus said could move mountains (Matt 17:20; 21:21; 1 Cor 13:2). Healings (literally, "charisms of healings") are actual healings of sicknesses or disabilities in response to prayer, as often demonstrated in Acts. The working of miracles, similarly, is a display of God's power that confirms the truth of the gospel (see Rom 15:19; 2 Cor 12:12; Gal 3:5; Heb 2:4). Discernment of spirits is the ability to recognize whether a particular spiritual phenomenon or utterance comes from the Holy Spirit, an evil spirit, or merely the human spirit.

Paul treats the remaining three "spiritual gifts"—prophecy, tongues, and interpretation of tongues—in more detail in 1 Cor 14. Paul's teaching implies that there are two forms of the gift of tongues. First, tongues can refer to a grace for prayer and praise in an unknown language (1 Cor 14:4; cf. Rom 8:26-27), a kind of "non-rational prayer of the heart."[16] Second, tongues can refer to a public message for the assembly. In the latter case, there is need for someone with the charism of interpretation of tongues to communicate its meaning to the assembly (1 Cor 14:5).

Finally, Paul places strongest emphasis on prophecy as the charism that is especially efficacious in building up the church (1 Cor 14:1-5). Prophecy is speech inspired by the Spirit, communicating a message that is not one's own but comes from God. It may include a disclosure concerning the future (cf. Acts 11:27-29) or the reading of hearts (1 Cor 14:25; cf. Acts 5:2-4), but more often it takes the form of encouragement and consolation (1 Cor 14:3) or conviction of sin (1 Cor 14:24). Prophecy is the only gift that appears every time Paul lists the charisms. Together with apostleship, it is foundational to the Church (Eph 2:20; cf. 1 Cor 12:28). Thus Paul often exhorts believers to strive for this gift: "earnestly desire the spiritual gifts, especially that you may prophesy" (1 Cor 14:1); "earnestly desire to prophesy" (1 Cor 14:39); "now I want you all to speak in tongues, but even more to prophesy" (1 Cor 14:4-5); "do not despise prophesying" (1 Thes 5:20).

The gift that holds first place in the hierarchy of charisms is apostleship, that charism which oversees and coordinates the harmonious interaction of all the other charisms (1 Cor 12:28; Eph 4:11). For Paul there is no opposition between office and charism, or between the institutional and spontaneous workings of the Spirit. The Church is built upon the foundation of apostles (representing its institutional dimension) and prophets (representing its charismatic dimension) (Eph 2:20). The Holy Spirit's activity in the Church is subject to the oversight and discernment of the Church's human authorities. Yet those appointed to pastor the Church must rely on the Holy Spirit and his spiritual gift of discernment, not merely on sound human reasoning. They are not masters of the charisms; their role is to order them to the good of the Church and its mission.

Paul also mentions charisms that are less obviously supernatural but no less important. These include service, teaching, exhortation, contribution, administration, and acts of mercy (Rom 12:6-8; cf. 1 Pet 2:10-11). In Eph 4:11-13 he lists categories of persons who have gifts of leadership in the Church: apostles, prophets, evangelists, pastors, and teachers. Paul also speaks of charisms of marriage and of celibacy (1 Cor 7:7); and of ordained ministry (1 Tim 4:14; 2 Tim 1:6). To these might be added other charisms mentioned elsewhere in Paul or in the New Testament: visions and revelations (Acts 9:10; 10:3; 11:5; 16:9; 18:9; 2 Cor 12:1-4), exorcisms (Acts 8:7; 16:18), intercession (Acts 12:5; 2 Cor 1:11), hospitality (Acts 16:15), song (1 Cor 14:26; Eph 5:19), voluntary poverty (1 Cor 13:3; Phil 4:12), and martyrdom (Acts 7:59-60; 12:2; 1 Cor 13:3).

To summarize these biblical reflections, the story of salvation is framed by the presence of the Holy Spirit, hovering over the primordial waters at creation and joining in the cry of the Bride at the end: "Come, Lord Jesus!" (Rev 22:17, 20). All Scripture points toward an eschatological outpouring of the Spirit, the fulfillment of God's plan to divinize human beings and renew all creation. This outpouring occurred definitively at Pentecost but is continually renewed throughout the time of the Church and will reach its consummation at the resurrection of the dead on the last day. Baptism in the Spirit as it is experienced in the

Church today can only be understood within this full biblical context.

3. Baptism in the Spirit in the Patristic Era

A question that naturally arises from the contemporary experience of baptism in the Spirit is: What precedent is there for this experience in Church history, and especially in the formative age of the Fathers? This question is founded in a conviction that an authentic grace of God cannot be without continuity with the Church's living tradition. Although a thorough investigation of the topic is beyond the scope of this book, here we provide some brief indications that the main features of baptism in the Spirit as experienced today were also present in the Church of the patristic era.[17]

3.1 Experiential Knowledge of God and of the Gift of Salvation

The writings of the Fathers of both East and West abound with references to the gift of the Spirit as an experienced reality. The Fathers did not view the Pentecost event described in Acts as something confined to the past but as something present and alive in the Church. St. Cyril of Jerusalem (c. 318-386), commenting on the Pentecost account and specifically the accusation that the disciples were "filled with new wine" (Acts 2:13), explained to a group of catechumens,

> They are not drunk in the way you might think. They are indeed drunk, but with the sober intoxication which kills sin and gives life to the heart and which is the opposite of

physical drunkenness. Drunkenness makes a person forget what he knows; this kind, instead, brings understanding of things that were not formerly known. They are drunk insofar as they have drunk the wine of that mystical vine which affirms, "I am the vine, you are the branches" (John 15:5).[18]

Cyril evidently expects that the catechumens themselves will experience something like this at their own baptism. St. Ambrose (c. 340–397), similarly, exclaims, "Let us drink with joy the sober intoxication of the Spirit!"[19] St. Augustine (354–430), preaching at a Pentecost liturgy, asks his congregation, "Is not the Holy Spirit being given now, brothers and sisters? Whoever thinks that is not worthy to receive him. Certainly he is being given now."[20] These pastors regard the gift of the Holy Spirit as the source of an overwhelming joy, a kind of spiritual inebriation. But unlike earthly drunkenness, the gift of the Spirit elevates rather than obscures understanding; it leads to holiness and self-sacrificing love rather than sin and degrading conduct.

The experience of the Spirit was regarded as integral to the sacraments of initiation. Christian initiation was a process that could last as long as two or three years, a time of intensive catechesis and deepening conversion in which the catechumens were brought into a living relationship with the Father through the Son and the Spirit. The process usually culminated in the celebration of baptism, confirmation and the Eucharist at the Easter Vigil liturgy. Drawing on the New Testament, several of the Fathers use the term "baptism in the Spirit" simply as a synonym for this sacramental incorporation into Christ.[21]

Many Fathers speak of Christian initiation as producing an experiential knowledge of the divine life into which one is baptized. In the East, Cyril tells candidates that when they are baptized, "You will grasp by experience the sublimity of the doctrines."[22] In the West, St. Hilary of Poitiers (c. 300–368) explains that the Spirit brings alive the doctrine of our adoptive sonship:

> [After Jesus' baptism] a voice from heaven speaks: "You are my beloved Son."... This was done so that we in our time might learn what has been fully realized in Christ. After the water-bath, the Holy Spirit rushes upon us from the gate of heaven, that we might bathe in the anointing of the heavenly glory, and that we might become sons of God through adoption spoken by the voice of the Father.[23]

St. Cyprian of Carthage (d. 258) gives eloquent testimony to the effects of the baptismal gift of the Spirit in his letter to Donatus, where he recounts what occurred at his own baptism:

> I went down into those life-giving waters, and all the stains of my past were washed away. I committed my life to the Lord; he cleansed my heart and filled me with the Holy Spirit. I was born again, a new man. Then in a most marvelous way all my doubts cleared up. I could now see what had been hidden from me before. I found I could do things that had previously been impossible. I saw that as long as I had been living according to my flesh I was at the mercy of sin and my course was set for death, but that by living according to my new birth in the Holy Spirit I had already begun to share God's eternal life.... We do not have

to toil and sweat to achieve our own perfection, nor are money and influence needed to obtain the gift of the Holy Spirit. It is freely given by God, always available for us to use. Just as the sun shines and the day brings light, the stream irrigates the soil and rain waters the earth, so the heavenly Spirit pours himself into us.[24]

It is evident that Christian initiation in the early Church was an inseparably ontological and experiential reality, bringing about a radical transformation of life.

3.2 The Charisms in the Early Church

There is evidence that abundant charisms were manifested in the early Church, including the "spiritual gifts" of 1 Corinthians 12. In the second century, St. Justin Martyr (c. 100-165) writes, "The prophetic gifts remain with us, even to the present time."[25] St. Irenaeus (c. 115-202) likewise observes, "We hear many of the brethren in the Church having prophetic charisms and speaking all kinds of tongues through the Spirit; and bringing the secrets of men to light for their good, and expounding the mysteries of God."[26] Irenaeus testifies to numerous miracles and other signs of the power of the Spirit:

> Those who are truly his disciples, receiving grace from him, perform [miracles] in his name for the well being of others, according to the gift that each one has received from him. For some truly drive out devils, so that those who have thus been cleansed from evil spirits frequently believe and join themselves to the Church. Others have foreknowledge of things to come: they see visions, and utter prophecies.

Still others heal the sick by laying their hands upon them, and they are made whole. Yes, moreover, the dead have even been raised up, and remained among us for many years. And what more shall I say? It is not possible to name the number of the gifts which the Church throughout the whole world has received from God, in the name of Jesus Christ who was crucified under Pontius Pilate, and which she exercises day by day for the benefit of the gentiles, not practicing deception on anyone, nor receiving any reward from them on account of such miracles. For as she has received freely from God, freely also she ministers.[27]

Several Fathers speak of the charisms as a normal accompaniment to the rite of Christian initiation. In his treatise *On Baptism* Tertullian (c. 160–225) writes:

> Therefore, you blessed ones, for whom the grace of God is waiting, when you come up from the most sacred bath of the new birth, when you spread out your hands for the first time in your mother's house with your brethren, ask your Father, ask your Lord, for the special gift of his inheritance: the distributed charisms.[28]

Cyril of Jerusalem, similarly, urges the baptismal candidates, "Let each one prepare himself to receive the heavenly gift of prophecy.... My final words, beloved ones, in this instruction are words of exhortation, urging all of you to prepare your souls for the reception of the heavenly charisms."[29] Hilary likewise exhorts Christians to exercise the charisms: "Let us make use of such generous gifts!"[30] Elsewhere he says:

> We who have been reborn through the sacrament of baptism experience intense joy when we feel within us the

first stirrings of the Holy Spirit. We begin to have insight into the mysteries of faith; we are able to prophesy and speak with wisdom. We become steadfast in hope and receive abundant gifts of healing. Demons are made subject to our authority. These gifts enter us like a gentle rain, and... little by little, they bear abundant fruit.[31]

St. Augustine (354-430), as is well known, changed his mind about the charisms. During the third and fourth centuries there had been a decline in the spiritual gifts, due in part to the rise of the Montanist heresy which was characterized by abuses and excesses in the use of charisms.[32] In reaction to this heresy, there was a tendency to avoid charismatic activity. In his early years Augustine wrote that although the charisms had been necessary in the apostolic age, now that the Church had reached maturity they were no longer needed. But later, after witnessing many miraculous healings in his own cathedral in Hippo, he realized that the Church does need these gifts. He later wrote in his *Retractions*,

> It is indeed true that the sick are not always healed.... But what I said should not be taken to mean that no miracles are believed to happen today in the name of Christ. For at the very time I wrote... a blind man in the city [of Milan] was given back his sight; and so many other things of this kind have happened, even in this present time, that it is not possible to know all of them or to count up all those we do have knowledge of.[33]

In *The City of God*, Augustine recounts many striking healings that he witnessed.[34] On one occasion, when a brother and sister were miraculously healed of a terrible ailment, he recounts the reaction of his congregation: "Such wonder rose up from men and women together that the exclamations and tears seemed as if they would never come to an end.... They shouted God's praises without words, but with such a noise that our ears could scarcely stand it."[35] In a sermon Augustine exhorts his congregation, "Our Lord Jesus Christ restored sight to the blind, raised Lazarus to life.... Let no one then, brethren, say that our Lord Jesus Christ does not do those things now and on this account prefer the former to the present ages of the Church."[36]

Closely related to the exercise of charisms was an awareness of the spiritual battle and the spiritual authority Christians have in the name of Jesus. St. Justin Martyr writes of numerous exorcisms done by Christians, bearing witness to the truth of the gospel:

> Jesus was born by the will of God the Father for the salvation of believers and the destruction of demons. And now you can learn this by what you see with your own eyes. For throughout the whole world and in your city [Rome] there are many demoniacs whom all the other exorcists, sorcerers, and magicians could not heal but whom our Christians have healed and do heal, disabling and casting out the demons who possessed them in the name of Jesus Christ who was crucified under Pontius Pilate.[37]

St. Athanasius's *Life of Saint Anthony* describes the spiritual combat in which the desert fathers were constantly engaged. Athanasius reports that Anthony delivered many people from demonic oppression, and was himself often tempted and attacked by evil spirits but overcame these attacks through faith and prayer.

3.3 Jubilation and the Gift of Tongues

After the second century there is little written about the gift of tongues. However, it does not necessarily follow that this gift disappeared from the Church. There is strong evidence that the biblical phenomenon of tongues continued, though with different terminology and perhaps in a different manner. Many of the Fathers speak of "jubilation," a form of praying and singing aloud without words, which seems to have close affinities with the gift of tongues as it is experienced today.[38] St. Augustine describes it thus:

> One who jubilates does not utter words, but a certain sound of joy without words: for it is the voice of the soul poured forth in joy, expressing, as far as possible, what it feels without reflecting on the meaning. Rejoicing in exultation, a man uses words that cannot be spoken and understood, but he simply lets his joy burst forth without words; his voice then appears to express a happiness so intense that he cannot explain it.[39]

Augustine urges his congregation to jubilate: "Rejoice and speak. If you cannot express your joy, jubilate: jubilation expresses your joy if you cannot speak. Let not your joy be silent."[40] St. Gregory the Great explains,

> But we call it *jubilus*, when we conceive such joy in the heart as we cannot give vent to by the force of words, and yet the triumph of the heart vents with the voice what it

cannot give forth by speech. Now the mouth is rightly said
to be filled with laughter, the lips with jubilation, since in
that eternal land, when the mind of the righteous is borne
away in transport, the tongue is lifted up in the song of
praise.[41]

This joy overflowing into wordless praise may be what Paul
refers to as "praying with the Spirit" and "singing with the
Spirit" (1 Cor 14:15) with "psalms and hymns and spiritual
songs" (Col 3:16; Eph 5:19). Worship in the early Church was
often quite expressive, with members of the congregation
spontaneously calling out words of praise and thanksgiving.
Sighs, tears, spontaneous songs, and clapping of hands were
common.[42] For centuries, jubilation with improvised melodies
was an ordinary part of the liturgy, forming part of the
foundation of medieval church music.[43]

From the examples given here, it is evident that the
experience of baptism in the Spirit in the Catholic
Charismatic Renewal, although its form and expression are in
some ways unique to our time, has deep roots in the Church's
tradition. It is beyond the scope of this document to discuss
the Spirit's charismatic activity in the Church from the end of
the patristic era to our own times. However, it is worth noting
that the full range of charisms experienced in the Renewal
have been manifested in various times and places, especially
the lives of saints such as Bernard, Francis of Assisi, Gertrude
the Great, Catherine of Siena, Vincent Ferrer, Ignatius of
Loyola, Francis Xavier, Teresa of Avila, John Vianney, John
Bosco, Pio of Pietrelcina, André Bessette, and many others.

Many aspects of the contemporary experience of baptism in the Spirit are also present in the Church's mystical and spiritual tradition, especially in the East. St. Symeon the New Theologian (949–1022), a Byzantine monk, wrote much about the "baptism of the Holy Spirit" as a profound mystical union with God that is accompanied by the gift of tears, sorrow for sins, and visions of God as light. The Russian St. Seraphim of Sarov (1759–1833) famously stated that "the aim of Christian life is the acquisition of the Holy Spirit." There is also abundant evidence of charisms in the Orthodox and Oriental churches, such as in the life of St. Takla Haymanot of Ethiopia and St. Nicetas of Novgorod, Russia.

Part III
Theological Reflection

The outpouring of the Spirit in the experience of the Catholic Charismatic Renewal, which has renewed the lives of so many Christians, calls for ongoing theological reflection. What is God's purpose in giving this grace? Is it for all Catholics? How does it relate to the life of the Church, and especially to the sacraments of initiation? What is the place of experience in the Christian life? This section will first briefly describe the theological understanding that has developed in the Renewal, then address some of the most common theological issues raised by baptism in the Spirit.

1. The Development of Understanding in the Catholic Charismatic Renewal

From its beginning in 1967, what came to be known as the Catholic Charismatic Renewal was founded in an event-experience that was called baptism in the Holy Spirit. Why was this terminology used? The first Catholics to receive this grace had been deeply marked by the recently concluded Second Vatican Council and by the "ecumenical dimension" in their initial experience. They adopted the same term that had been used in the Pentecostal movement, which had in turn been adapted from Scripture (see Part II, section 2 above). They understood these beginnings as a fulfillment of Pope John XXIII's prayer for the Council, asking for "a new Pentecost." The link between "baptism in the Spirit" and the Pentecost event, both in the New Testament and in contemporary experience, seemed to confirm the appropriateness of this term.

The first Catholics caught up in this unexpected grace of baptism in the Spirit quickly understood that this grace was to be understood in the context of the profound renewal of Catholic life that was the heart and goal of Vatican II. They had an intense impulse to communicate this grace more widely in the Catholic Church and a clear conviction that this grace was for the renewal of the whole Church. Their strong ecclesial sense was one major difference from the origins of the charismatic movement in the Protestant communions. Catholics baptized in the Spirit recognized the need for this movement to be received into the Catholic Church under the guidance of the pope and the bishops.

Early on it was recognized that this outpouring of the Spirit necessitated a thorough theological reflection, including an examination of the terminology of "baptism in the Spirit," in the light of Catholic tradition. The promotion of this theological reflection was a major concern of Cardinal Léon-Joseph Suenens of Belgium, who took part in a meeting of theologians and leaders held at Grottaferrata, Italy, in 1973 and then oversaw the production of the Malines documents. The first Malines document, *Theological and Pastoral Orientations on the Catholic Charismatic Renewal*,[1] examined the emerging reality of the movement in the light of Catholic tradition and theology and made a number of recommendations. The authors included theologians who had already begun the effort to articulate an authentically Catholic theology of baptism in the Spirit.

The first Malines document recognized that various terms were already being used to describe what was popularly being called baptism in the Holy Spirit. In effect, alternative phrases were being adopted by 1972 as the Charismatic Renewal spread beyond North America into other cultures and language groups. One reason for seeking an alternative phrase was the concern to avoid confusion between baptism in the Spirit and the sacrament of baptism. So, for example, the most common usage in French-speaking countries is *effusion de l'Esprit*, and in Italian *effusione dello Spirito*. The same is true in Spain (*efusion del Espiritu*) and Portugal (*efusão no Espírito*), although in Latin America the more common terms are *bautismo en el Espiritu* and *batismo no Espírito*. In Polish both *wylanie Ducha Świętego* (outpouring of the Holy Spirit) and *chrzest w Duchu Świętym* (baptism in the Holy Spirit) are used, as in German *Geisttaufe* (Spirit-baptism) and *Erneuerung im Heiligen Geist* (renewal in the Holy Spirit). In some areas other terms such as "new Pentecost" or "personal Pentecost" are popular. By contrast, the English-speaking world has almost universally retained the term *baptism in the Spirit*. When the baptismal language and imagery is used, a clear explanation of its relationship to sacramental baptism becomes necessary (see section 5.1 below).

The advantage of the term "effusion in the Holy Spirit" is that it avoids any suggestion of two baptisms, one in water and one in Spirit, which would devalue the sacrament of baptism. It should be noted, however, that there is no real equivalent for "effusion" in English.[2] On the other hand, the advantage of "baptism in the Holy Spirit" is that it preserves the language used by both John the Baptist and Jesus for the Holy Spirit's completion of the work of redemption, with its direct link to the Pentecost event. It also expresses the particularity of what is experienced in the Renewal, whereas "effusion" applies more broadly to any action of the Spirit in the Christian life.

While "baptism in the Holy Spirit" affirms an affinity with the wider Pentecostal and charismatic movements that commonly use this term, Catholics must avoid a misguided "two-baptism" explanation. The use of the baptismal terminology may also arouse additional pastoral concerns in situations where there are Pentecostal or charismatic groups with some questionable emphases.

Each of the terminological traditions has its own legitimacy and its own limitations, linked to different cultural and ecclesial contexts. The fact that different terms continue to be used is an indication of the richness of the reality, which cannot be fully captured in any single phrase.

2. The Heart of Baptism in the Spirit

The characteristics of baptism in the Spirit described in Part I demonstrate that baptism in the Spirit is not a phenomenon on the margins of Christian life. It concerns the heart of the gospel, the missions of the Son and the Holy Spirit from the Father. The Lord Jesus is at the center of the charismatic witness—the incarnate, crucified, and risen Lord Jesus who was conceived, indwelt and empowered by the Holy Spirit, and who will come in glory. It is this all-embracing Trinitarian perspective to which the words of Benedict XVI recall the Church: Jesus is "the One who came to baptize humanity in the Holy Spirit."[3]

Through baptism in the Spirit Pentecost is made present and alive in the Church today. To be baptized in the Holy Spirit is to be filled with the Love that eternally flows between Father and Son in the Holy Trinity, a love that changes people at the deepest level of their being and makes them capable of loving God in return. Christians thus experience Christ's paschal mystery as a present source of grace and power, and come to know "what is the breadth and length and height and depth... the love of Christ that surpasses knowledge" (Eph 3:18-19). They cry out from their hearts, "Abba, Father" (Rom 8:15; Gal 4:6), "Jesus is Lord" (1 Cor 12:3), and "Come, Lord Jesus" (Rev 22:16, 20). There is a deeper communion with the Persons of the Holy Trinity and an experience of being raised up to our God-given inheritance in Christ, an initial taste of the future resurrection. This is at the heart of the theological meaning of baptism as presented by Paul: "We were buried therefore with him by baptism into death, so that as Christ was raised from the dead by the glory of the Father, we too might walk in newness of life" (Rom 6:4). God "raised us up with him, and made us sit with him in the heavenly places in Christ Jesus" (Eph 2:6; cf. Col 3:3). The Holy Spirit empowers one to put on "the mind of Christ"—to think like him and love like him (Rom 13:14; 1 Cor 2:16; Phil 2:5) and thus to do the works he did (John 14:12). These things are true in principle for every baptized Christian, but through baptism in the Spirit they become an experienced reality. This in turn leads to victory over sin, authority over the temptations and deceits of the evil one, and growth in virtue through union with the risen Jesus.[4]

The charisms that characterize the Charismatic Renewal flow from the surrender to Jesus that is at the heart of baptism in the Spirit. The charisms are manifestations of the sovereignty of the risen Lord that are meant to be received gratefully, fostered, and used generously. This is not to say that the charisms cannot be abused, but their abuse entails the grave danger of following spirits other than the Holy Spirit. In the context of Church history, the experience of charisms in the Renewal today is new in that, first, the full range of charisms described by St. Paul in 1 Corinthians is present as part of the Holy Spirit's endowment of the Church. Second, the charisms are in principle available to every Christian rather than being largely limited to clergy or religious, or those who have practiced years of ascetical discipline. They are understood not as special graces for very holy people but as public gifts that equip the body of Christ to fulfil its mission. The exercise of charisms by millions of Catholics poses new demands for the Church. There is a need to further develop a theology of the charisms and a body of spiritual and pastoral wisdom concerning their use.[5]

From its nature as a yielding to the Spirit of God, baptism in the Spirit cannot be made dependent on a particular sign of its reception. For this reason, the doctrine that speaking in tongues is a necessary sign of baptism in the Spirit is not acceptable in the Catholic tradition. However, the gift of tongues is widely diffused and is often the first charism experienced upon receiving baptism in the Spirit. Prayer in tongues can play a significant role in opening a person to the influence of the Spirit and thus to the whole realm of spiritual gifts.

3. Theology and Experience

In the New Testament and the early Church, it was taken for granted that the gift of the Spirit was not merely a doctrine but a fact of experience. Baptism in the Spirit thus raises the question of the value and role of experience in the Christian life. Catholic tradition has always recognized the importance of the experiential dimension of the spiritual life,[6] although the role experience has sometimes been subjected to theological distortions. Understood rightly, experience is fully human because it involves all the human faculties in integral unity (the five senses, the imagination, emotions, intellect and will). Experience should not be reduced to feelings and emotions, which would make it merely subjective.

Christian experience is not a vague, subjective phenomenon that can be attributed to any of various causes. It is experience of an objective reality: God's gift of himself to us through the cross and resurrection of Jesus Christ and the outpouring of the Holy Spirit. Christian experience is always linked with the preaching and teaching of the faith. It occurs through hearing the word of God, accepting it in faith, and participating in the sacramental and liturgical life of the Church. Although we do not experience God directly in this life, we experience created realities in which God is present and acting (participating in the liturgy, hearing good preaching, praying, exercising charisms, encountering holy people, being moved by Christian music and art).

What difference does baptism in the Spirit make in this context? Baptism in the Spirit is a revelation of the Father's love and of the truth that "Jesus is Lord" which profoundly deepens Christian experience. At the same time it is a surrender to Jesus' lordship through the Holy Spirit, so that one is increasingly "led by the Spirit of God" (Rom 8:14). The "pilot of the ship" is no longer the individual, but the Holy Spirit. This is truly life in the Spirit, a life that leads to exultation in praise and worship, joyful witness and profound communion with God and with others. Although it has an experiential dimension, God's action in us is always greater than that which we perceive.

It is a mistake to imagine an opposition between Christian experience and the sacraments. The sacraments, through which we are brought into contact with Christ's paschal mystery, form the foundation for Christian experience. Even if we come to a new experience of God's action in a non-sacramental context, its full meaning is embodied in the sacraments and liturgy of the Church. Christian maturity is a deepening personal integration between God's action in the sacraments and God's action in the believer.

4. The Institutional and Charismatic Dimensions of the Church

Summing up an insight of Vatican Council II, Pope John Paul II stated that "the *institutional dimension* and the *charismatic dimension...* are co-essential to the divine constitution of the Church founded by Jesus, because they both help to make the mystery of Christ and his saving work present in the world."[7] The institutional and charismatic are two complementary ways in which the Spirit works, which "contribute, although differently, to the life, renewal and sanctification of God's People."[8] The institutional (or hierarchical) dimension refers to all that was instituted by Jesus during his earthly life, including his choice of the Twelve apostles; his conferral of authority upon them; his command to preach the gospel, to baptize, and to celebrate the Eucharist "in memory of me"; the power to forgive sins; and other structural elements that belong to the deposit of faith. The charismatic dimension refers to the gifts poured out spontaneously at Pentecost and afterward by the Holy Spirit, who freely distributes his graces when and where he wills.[9] The institutional is passed down from generation to generation and belongs to the permanent visible structure of the Church. The charismatic is given by the Lord in an unpredictable way and cannot be codified. Baptism in the Spirit, as a manifestation of the spontaneous working of the Spirit, belongs to the charismatic dimension, but at the same time it brings new life and dynamism to the institutional dimension grounded in the sacraments.

The Church's perennial need to integrate the charismatic workings of the Spirit with the institutional structure is seen already in the New Testament. The Holy Spirit initiated a significant new initiative in the Church, Paul's mission to the gentiles (Acts 13:2-3), but Paul took care to "lay before [the apostles]... the gospel which I preached among the gentiles"

(Gal 2:2). When a major pastoral question arose concerning the circumcision of gentiles, Paul and Barnabas submitted it to "the apostles and elders" of Jerusalem for discernment (Acts 15:2), then accepted their conclusions. The charismatic workings of the Spirit can never be independent of the ordained ministry. Without the institutional dimension there is no coherent tradition, no visible body into which the charismatic is poured. The charismatic dimension needs the institutional as a safeguard from deception and error, so that it can bear long-term fruit for the body of Christ. On the other hand, the institutional dimension needs the charismatic for the full creativity of the Holy Spirit to be manifested in the Church in every age and for the Church to be constantly reminded of her dependence on the risen Lord and his Spirit.[10]

5. Baptism in the Spirit and the Sacraments of Initiation

From the beginning of the Catholic Charismatic Renewal, theologians have sought to understand and articulate the relationship between baptism in the Spirit and the sacraments, especially the sacraments of initiation.[11] There have been two primary ways of describing baptism in the Spirit: as an actualization of the grace of baptism and confirmation, and as a new sending of the Spirit.

5.1 An Actualization of Baptism and Confirmation

Baptism in the Spirit is often described as a "coming alive," "renewal," or "release" of the grace of sacramental baptism and confirmation. These expressions recognize that today "baptism in the Spirit" usually refers to an experience *subsequent* to the sacraments of initiation, whereas in the early Church "baptism in the Spirit" referred to sacramental initiation and its effects as a single ontological-experiential reality. The normal effects of baptism and confirmation, as seen in Scripture and the Church Fathers, are intimate communion with the triune God flowing forth in a transformed life, in prayer and praise, and in a zeal to share the gospel with others, often with the manifestation of charisms.[12] As Christianity developed and infant baptism became the norm, it became increasingly possible to receive the sacraments without these subjective effects.[13] In such a situation (which is typical today) strong catechesis and formation are necessary to help a person develop a living faith and personally appropriate the new life he or she has received.

Even in the case of young people or adults receiving baptism or confirmation, although grace is objectively conferred, the life-transforming effects of the sacraments may be lacking for various reasons.[14] According to the *Catechism of the Catholic Church*, confirmation "in a certain way perpetuates the grace of Pentecost in the Church" (1288). Yet it must be admitted that often today this does not occur in any vital or perceptible way. Various factors such as inadequate preaching of the word of God, lukewarm faith, unrepented sin, insufficient preparation, lack of understanding of the reality of the sacraments, a secular mindset, or psychological or spiritual obstacles can hinder the sacraments from achieving their full fruitfulness.[15]

In this light, what occurs in baptism in the Spirit is an actualization of the sacraments of initiation, a "fanning into flame" the gift already received (cf. 2 Tim 1:6). Here the word of God plays a crucial role, as those preparing for baptism in the Spirit often receive a fuller preaching of what had not been previously conveyed to them. The regeneration and divine life received in baptism and confirmation become a matter of living experience.

If baptism in the Spirit is the normal development of the Christian life that begins with the sacraments of initiation, it follows that this grace is not something unique to the Charismatic Renewal. It is present in different forms in the lives of many other Catholics without reference to the specific terminology or style of the Renewal. The special calling of the Renewal is to name this grace, to propose an ecclesial context and a specific pedagogy for receiving it, and to foster the full development of its fruits.

5.2 A New Work of the Spirit

Baptism in the Spirit has alternatively been described as a new sending of the Spirit into a person's life. This viewpoint emphasizes that although baptism in the Spirit is inherently related to the sacraments, it cannot be described solely as a release of dormant sacramental graces through the removal of obstacles. The idea of release expresses one dimension of baptism in the Spirit: the coming forth into consciousness and effective power of that which was already within. But it does not address another aspect: the Spirit of God coming in a new way into a person's life and bestowing new gifts. Baptism in the Spirit is an action of the Holy Spirit—in some sense a distinct "mission" of the Spirit—and not a human work. It involves not only the "already given" but the "new from above."

Moreover, people's actual experience of baptism in the Spirit varies widely, although there is a common core as described in Part I above. For some people, there is a sudden and dramatic change; for others, there is a more gradual change over time. For many, baptism in the Spirit constitutes their adult conversion—a personal encounter with Christ that radically transforms them and sets them on the path of discipleship for the first time. For others, conversion has already occurred and baptism in the Spirit constitutes a fuller release of the Spirit and his charisms, especially in preparation for a new mission or task to which God is calling them. St. Thomas Aquinas refers to such a decisively new work of the Spirit in a Christian's life when he writes,

> There is an invisible sending [of the Holy Spirit] also in respect to an advance in virtue or an increase of grace.... Such an invisible sending is especially to be seen in that kind of increase of grace whereby a person moves forward to some new act or new state of grace: as, for instance, when a person moves forward into the grace of working miracles, or of prophecy, or out of the burning love of God offers his life as a martyr, or renounces all of his possessions, or undertakes some other such arduous thing.[16]

Although the Spirit often comes in response to prayer, he comes in a way that is gratuitous, mysterious, and uniquely tailored to each individual. Thus one cannot make a particular way of receiving baptism in the Spirit mandatory or normative. This grace remains at its core a sovereign gift to bless the whole Church, freely given and freely received.

6. Is Baptism in the Spirit for Every Christian?

This key question has been the subject of debate. Many of those in the charismatic renewal, both Protestants and Catholics, are firmly convinced that the grace of baptism in the Spirit is for every member of the Church. In the early years of the Catholic Charismatic Renewal this was sometimes expressed by a comparison with the liturgical renewal: just as the liturgical renewal was for the whole Church and destined to disappear into a liturgically renewed Church, so the charismatic renewal would disappear into a charismatically renewed Church. Others, including bishops, were hesitant before such a claim, and saw the Charismatic Renewal as one of the many new ecclesial movements, each with its own charisms, within the communion of the universal Church. Pope John Paul II related particular charisms to the universal Church in his teaching on lay associations of the faithful: "All of us, Pastors and lay faithful, have the duty to promote and nourish stronger bonds and mutual esteem, cordiality and collaboration among the various forms of lay associations. Only in this way can the richness of the gifts and charisms that the Lord offers us bear their fruitful contribution in building the common house."[17]

Important truths are being expressed in both positions. As an organized movement with its own structures and patterns of initiation and formation, the Charismatic Renewal is one ecclesial movement among many, to which the words of John

Paul II cited above fully apply. But baptism in the Spirit is for all the baptized insofar as it is coming alive of sacramental baptism and confirmation.

Similarly, charisms as such are for the whole Church, since they belonged to the ministry of Jesus and were part of what he passed on to the Church through the Twelve.[18] However, the particular forms that these gifts take in various times and settings cannot be made normative for any person or group. One cannot say that any one charism is for all Christians, since they are freely given as the Spirit wills. This last point also applies to those aspects of the spirituality of the Charismatic Renewal that represent a particular way of responding to the grace of baptism in the Spirit but cannot be considered the only way.

7. Should Non-Baptized Persons Receive Prayer for Baptism in the Spirit?

The previous section gives rise to a related question: should non-baptized persons be prayed with for baptism in the Spirit? Scripture records one instance where the Pentecostal outpouring of the Spirit occurred prior to baptism (Acts 10:44-48). However, Luke makes clear that this event was a unique intervention by God in order to make evident that salvation in Christ is for gentiles as well as Jews. Elsewhere in Acts, and throughout Christian tradition, baptism and confirmation are the normal means by which the gift of the Spirit is imparted.

Although God is free to give the Spirit as he wills even apart from the sacraments, his people are obliged to respect the ordinary channels of grace that have been established by Christ. People should normally be prayed with for baptism in the Spirit only after undergoing conversion to Christ and receiving the sacrament of baptism. However, this does not preclude praying with non-baptized persons for the Spirit's light and grace to help them along the path of conversion. In some cases, people are willing to come to a Life in the Spirit Seminar or similar course before they are ready to enter the RCIA process. In such cases, leaders can seek the Lord's wisdom as to how to pray for these people and ensure that there is good follow-up inviting them to the fullness of Christian initiation (see Part IV, section 3 below).

8. Can One Be Baptized in the Spirit More Than Once?

Baptism in the Spirit, as it is usually understood, is a new encounter with the Spirit in one's life, an experience that creates a distinct "before" and "after." In this sense it is a unique event, like Pentecost in the early Church. However, this does not preclude the possibility of renewed comings of the Spirit, as also occurred in the early Church (Acts 4:31).[19] From time to time all Christians need and can pray for a new outpouring of the Spirit, especially in view of new circumstances such as marriage, a call to an apostolate, an illness, and so on, which require new gifts of the Spirit. There is also the possibility of backsliding, in which case there is need for repentance and renewal. The Church believes that all Christians have received the Holy Spirit in baptism, yet in her prayers she teaches us always to implore him anew: "Come, Holy Spirit!"

Part IV
Pastoral Issues

Baptism in the Spirit is most fruitful in settings where there is good pastoral accompaniment and a process of sound formation and integration into the life of the Church. This section will provide some guidelines for overseeing the reception and living out of baptism in the Spirit and will address some of the related pastoral issues.

1. Preparation for Baptism in the Spirit

Good preparation helps ensure that people experience baptism in the Spirit not as an isolated, superficial event but as the impetus for a life of ongoing conversion, holiness, and mission. Preparation also helps people open their hearts fully to the grace of God and ground their experience in the faith and life of the Church.

Many Catholics have never received a solid formation. Moreover, as Pope John Paul II observed, many Catholics have been baptized and catechized without being sufficiently *evangelized*, that is, without hearing the basic proclamation of the gospel in a way that brought them to a personal encounter with Christ and conversion of heart.[1] Cardinal Stanisław

Rylko, president of the Pontifical Council for the Laity, has noted that today's culture often "produces individuals whose Christian identity is weak and confused; faith is little more than a routine practice often influenced by a dangerous syncretism.... Membership in the Church, often superficial and distracted, fails to impact their choices and behavior in any significant way."[2] In addition, many individuals have been wounded by family dysfunction and other effects of the culture of death; thus inner healing is often needed before people can open themselves fully to the grace of the Holy Spirit.

Formation, particularly through preaching of the word of God, is crucial for providing a context and explanation for what people experience. Vatican II taught that God's plan "is realized by deeds and words having an inner unity; the deeds wrought by God in the history of salvation manifest and confirm the teaching and realities signified by the words, while the words proclaim the deeds and clarify the mystery contained in them" (*Dei Verbum*, 2). This principle also holds true for baptism in the Spirit and every work of God in human life. There is generally a direct correlation between what is preached and what is experienced. Sound preaching and teaching open people to being touched by God and equip them to properly interpret what they experience. Conversely, the experience of God makes the doctrines of the faith come alive in a personal and existential way.

In the early days of the Charismatic Renewal, the Life in the Spirit Seminar was developed as a way to prepare Catholics to receive baptism in the Spirit. The seminar is usually in the form of a six- or seven-week course but can also take place during a weekend or even in a single day, or in a longer format (10 weeks or more) that includes further evangelization or catechesis.[3] The Life in the Spirit Seminar works best for Catholics who already know the basics of the faith. For people who have had little or no faith formation, it may be advisable to begin with an evangelistic program that proclaims the basic gospel message.

The personal testimonies of people whose lives have been transformed by the Holy Spirit are an important part of formation. Such testimonies can awaken expectant faith and help people grasp concretely how the Spirit acts in our lives.

It is recommended that formation for baptism in the Holy Spirit include the components listed below.

1.1 The Love of God the Father

"God's love has been poured into our hearts through the Holy Spirit that has been given to us" (Rom 5:5). Many people find it difficult to accept God's love, both because of experiences of rejection in their past and because of the fallen human tendency to think we need to earn God's love. Thus an important part of preparation for baptism in the Spirit is clear preaching on God's personal, unconditional, tender love for each person—a love that infinitely surpasses anything we could earn or deserve. This includes an explanation of the basic gospel kerygma, that is, how God has manifested his love for us: "God shows his love for us in that while we were yet sinners Christ died for us" (Rom 5:8; see 1 John 4:10). The knowledge of God's love, imparted by the Holy Spirit, changes a person at the deepest level of the heart and becomes the foundation for a wholehearted response of love for him in return.

1.2 The Lordship of Jesus

"In your hearts reverence Christ as Lord" (1 Pet 3:15). Formation teaching should prepare those who have never done so to consciously invite Jesus into their hearts as Savior and Lord. This includes explanation of the reality of sin and the good news of forgiveness of sins and reconciliation with God through the cross of Christ. Jesus is our friend and brother; he understands all our weaknesses and temptations, and is always with us in all the joys and sorrows of life. He has truly conquered sin, and by the power of his cross we can resist our sinful tendencies and live a new life as sons and daughters of God. The recognition of Jesus' sovereign authority over all things (Acts 10:36) gives people peace, freedom and a new desire to submit their lives to him. Teaching should help people joyfully embrace the call to radical discipleship, even though it means taking up the cross and going against the current of the world.

1.3 The Power of the Holy Spirit

"You will receive power when the Holy Spirit comes upon you" (Acts 1:8). Baptism in the Spirit brings about an interior revolution: instead of Christian life consisting of our efforts to grow in holiness, which God comes to strengthen and crown, there is a deep realization that "by grace we have been saved" (Eph 2:5) and apart from Christ we can do nothing.[4] This awareness of our spiritual poverty leads not to discouragement but to confident trust in the Lord: "Not by might, nor by power, but by my Spirit, says the LORD of hosts" (Zech 4:6). Good teaching presents the Spirit's power as, first, a power for sanctification, and second, a power equipping us to be witnesses of Christ, as Jesus himself was empowered by the Spirit for his earthly ministry (Luke 3:21-22; 4:18-20). As a person learns to be led by the Spirit, the Spirit brings forth the fruit of holiness: "Love, joy, peace, patience, kindness, goodness, faithfulness, gentleness, self-control" (Gal 5:22-23). In this regard it is helpful to draw on examples from the lives of the saints. There should also be guidance on how to become aware of and obedient to the quiet inner promptings of the Spirit.

1.4 Repentance, Forgiveness, and the Spiritual Battle

"Whenever you stand praying, forgive, if you have anything against anyone, so that your Father who is in heaven may in turn forgive you your trespasses" (Mark 11:25). To open ourselves fully to the Holy Spirit, there is need for repentance from sin and forgiveness of anyone who has offended us, which is itself a grace of God.

Baptism in the Spirit often brings a keener awareness of sin and the spiritual battle, as Jesus himself was led into the desert to be tempted by Satan immediately after his baptism (Mark 1:12-13). Formation should include practical instruction on how to resist the tactics of the evil one (his temptations, attempts to frighten, lies, accusations) and on putting on the armor of God (Eph 6:12). Demons are fallen angels that have no power except as permitted by God's providence, and Christ has won the definitive victory over them on the cross. Teaching on the spiritual battle should never arouse fear of demons nor an unhealthy preoccupation with them, but rather a zeal to resist sin and a confidence in the Lord's victory.

In parts of the world where recourse to witchcraft or occult activity is widespread, there may be need for prayers of deliverance or, in extreme cases, an exorcism performed by an authorized diocesan exorcist. Any signs of demonic activity must be addressed before there is prayer for baptism in the Spirit. Participants may be led in a clear renunciation of Satan and all his works, for which the renewal of baptismal vows in the Easter Vigil liturgy provides a good model. Teachings may also include an explanation of Jesus' saving work in this way: Jesus saves us 1) from all personal sin; 2) from all wounds caused by others; 3) from all evil spirits; 4) from sickness; 5) from death.[5]

Inviting people to receive the sacrament of reconciliation before prayer for baptism in the Spirit is highly recommended. People should be encouraged to avail themselves regularly of the sacraments and other means given by the Church to resist sin and Satan (for instance, sacramentals like holy water).

1.5 The Charisms

"Make love your aim, and earnestly desire the spiritual gifts" (1 Cor 14:1). Although charisms are given to each member of the body of Christ (1 Cor 12:7), few Catholics are aware that they have charisms or know how to use them. Preparation for baptism in the Spirit should include teaching on the charisms the Spirit bestows (see Part II, section 2.3 above) and how to receive and exercise them. Charisms are distinct from the sanctifying gifts given to all in baptism (cf. Isa 11:1-2), which complete and perfect the virtues.[6] They are also distinct from human talents, although they can sometimes build on human talents such as teaching or hospitality. Charisms are distributed in different measure to different people and are to be used in service to others for building up the body of Christ. The gift of tongues is often, though not always, the first charism received. Because it is a simple way of yielding to the Spirit, it can be a doorway to other charisms. However, as noted above, tongues should not be portrayed as a necessary sign of baptism in the Spirit.

1.6 Continued Growth

"They devoted themselves to the apostles' teaching and fellowship, to the breaking of bread and the prayers" (Acts 2:42). If baptism in the Spirit is to be a lasting grace, there must be a commitment to practices that build a strong spiritual life. Just as in the early Church, these include teaching, fellowship, the sacraments, and prayer.

Formation should help people develop a habit of daily prayer and of Scripture reading in the form of *lectio divina*.

Baptism in the Spirit gives a powerful impetus for the formation of community. Ideally, the Life in the Spirit Seminar leads to the formation of small faith-sharing groups that meet regularly. Small groups give people a context to develop Christian friendships; to share their joys, sorrows, and burdens; and to learn to pray over one another and support one another in the call to holiness. Such groups are a powerful antidote to the loneliness and depersonalization of contemporary society. Indeed, it is impossible to live the Christian life without community in some form.

The participants should also be given opportunities to continue to deepen their knowledge of the faith and of the saints and spiritual traditions of the Church. There is need for formation in the Church's moral teaching, especially in view of the many onslaughts of secular culture. The theology of the body, Pope John Paul's catecheses on human love in the divine plan, is particularly helpful for giving people a vision of the beauty of God's plan for human life.

Finally, people should continue to nurture their spiritual life by participating regularly and wholeheartedly in the sacrament of reconciliation and in the Eucharist, "the source and summit of the Christian life" (*Catechism of the Catholic Church*, 1324).

1.7 Mission

"Freely you have received, freely give" (Matt 10:8). God's love remains alive in a person only to the degree it is given away, as water that has no outlet will stagnate. Formation teaching helps people to recognize how they are sent forth by the Spirit: each person has been given a mission by God, a unique and indispensable part to play in the mission of the body of Christ.[7] They are called to leave the "upper room" and go out into the world, bearing the good news.

As recent popes have emphasized, all Catholics are called to evangelize.[8] All are called to be living witnesses to Christ both in word and in deed, in the family, in the workplace, and in society at large. Lay people in particular have the task of transforming the culture by bringing the light of Christ into every aspect of society. Baptism in the Spirit often brings a new dynamism and creativity for this task, as people are awakened to the fact that they have been gifted and called to be heralds of the gospel.

Sharing in the mission of the Church includes putting oneself and one's gifts at the service of others, often in humble ways. It means being alert to the needs of others, especially the materially or spiritually poor, and doing the works of mercy—providing food, shelter, clothing, and encouragement; interceding for others; praying for healing and deliverance; bearing witness to gospel values and working for peace and justice in society.

2. Praying for Baptism in the Spirit

Prayer for baptism in the Holy Spirit usually takes place in the context of a prayer group or community, among brothers and sisters who have themselves experienced baptism in the Spirit. As Cardinal Paul Josef Cordes has pointed out, "Here the *communio*-dimension of God's Spirit comes to expression. He usually chooses the path of mediation through brothers and sisters in faith, that is, through the faith community of the Church."[9]

The prayer for baptism in the Spirit is usually preceded by a brief teaching to stir up faith, explain how to yield to the Spirit and his charisms, and encourage the appropriate dispositions of trust, peace, simplicity, and joy. There may be a reading of Scripture passages such as Mark 16:15-18; Luke 11:9-13; John 14:16; Acts 2:1-4; 4:24-31; 10:44-46. There is then a renewal of baptismal promises, led by a priest or deacon if possible using the standard liturgical form, and a prayer of personal commitment to Jesus Christ. In this way people open themselves to the action of the Holy Spirit through a free decision, a step of conversion in which they surrender themselves wholly to Jesus without setting any limits on God's action.[10]

The leaders or members of the faith community then pray for each individual for baptism in the Holy Spirit. This prayer is usually accompanied by the gesture of laying hands on the person's head or shoulder. "The laying on of hands is not a sacramental rite, although this gesture is often present in the celebration of the Sacraments. It is, rather, an everyday gesture that the Judeo-Christian Tradition has always known and practiced."[11] The laying on of hands signifies that brothers and sisters are united with the individual, walking shoulder to shoulder. The prayer is marked by simplicity and expectant faith, trusting in Jesus' promise: "If you then, who are evil, know how to give good gifts to your children, how much more will the heavenly Father give the Holy Spirit to those who ask him!" (Luke 11:13). Leaders should make clear that the action of the Spirit is a free gift of God, not dependent on the holiness or giftedness of those who are praying. There should not be any attempt to produce particular phenomena or to control the work of the Spirit. Since baptism in the Spirit belongs to the charismatic dimensions of the Church, care should be taken not to turn prayer for baptism in the Spirit into a quasi-liturgical rite, but to leave the Holy Spirit free to move as he wills.

People's experience of being prayed over for baptism in the Spirit will vary widely. For some, there is intense emotion, sometimes of joy accompanied by tears. Some have an overwhelming sense of God's love; others a deep sense of peace; some have no discernable reaction at all. In some, there is an immediate manifestation of charisms; in others, there is not. Some experience spiritual changes later, in the days or weeks following the prayer. Participants should be helped to understand that the Spirit's presence is not measured by emotion or feeling. On the other hand, there can be obstacles within a person, for instance, fears, unrepented sin, or inner wounds, that hinder the full release of the Spirit. Mature leadership is essential for discerning what is happening and assisting each person with sensitivity and respect.

Following the prayer for baptism in the Spirit, it is good to have a time of worship and thanksgiving, during which all the participants are encouraged to yield to the Spirit's charisms, particularly prophecy, words of knowledge, praying or singing in tongues, and spontaneous praise. To encourage the exercise of gifts does not mean to force them; the freedom of each person is to be respected. This time of communal worship can be a good setting for people to gain courage and take small steps in learning to use and discern the charisms. As with any gift, it takes time and practice for a person to learn to exercise a charism rightly. Mistakes will be made. But if there is a spirit of humility and docility, mistakes will lead to progress.

Finally, it must be remembered that while human means of preparation are useful and necessary, God himself is not bound by them. Some people are baptized in the Spirit spontaneously, without any human intervention. This sometimes occurs during the liturgy or in personal prayer, at a retreat or conference, or in the most unexpected times and places. In such cases, there is still a need for sound, ongoing formation in order for the gift of God to take root and bear fruit in the person's life. Those who lead preparation programs must remember that their task is not to produce but to assist the work of the Spirit, who sovereignly acts in each person's life as he wills.

3. Follow-up to Baptism in the Spirit

From beginning to end, preparation teachings should make clear that baptism in the Spirit is not a one-time event but the beginning of a journey whose goal is the renewal of the whole of Christian life. The gift of the Spirit is not static but is meant to grow and bring forth the mature fruit of holiness.[12] This requires that after prayer for baptism in the Spirit, further opportunities be provided for people to grow in the spiritual life. These should include ongoing study of Scripture and of Catholic teaching, especially for lay people who have a charism for popular preaching but who lack theological formation.

People newly baptized in the Spirit also need both encouragement and opportunities to practice exercising the spiritual gifts. Instruction should be given on how to use the gifts in accord with their purpose, which is to build up the body of Christ. It may be helpful to explain the following basic criteria of discernment. The exercise of an authentic charism

- focuses attention on Jesus Christ and gives glory to him, rather than drawing attention to the individual;

- in the case of a "word gift" like prophecy, is fully consistent with Catholic teaching;[13]
- contributes to the building up of the body of Christ in love;
- avoids an overemphasis on method or technique, as if a successful outcome such as healing is due to the individual's expertise rather than the free gift of the Holy Spirit;
- avoids anything resembling occult practices, such as conversing with demons, and is marked by simplicity and humility, trusting the Lord to act as he wills;
- is marked by a spirit of obedience, both to the pastors of the Church and to those in legitimate authority in the local setting.

4. Integration into the Life of the Church

The first fruit of Christ's passion and resurrection and the outpouring of the Spirit at Pentecost was the birth of the Church. Then as now, the Christian life cannot be lived alone but only in communion with the body of believers established by Christ. Recognizing this, the Charismatic Renewal has always sought to be in full communion with the Church and her pastors. As discussed in Part III, section 6 above, in a certain sense the Charismatic Renewal is a movement among other movements in the Church, with its own particular style and spirituality. But in another sense the Renewal is unique, in that it is the bearer of a grace that belongs to the whole Church and is meant for the renewal of the whole Church.[14] This twofold reality creates a special responsibility for leaders and participants in the renewal. On the one hand, they are called to treasure and foster the grace of baptism in the Spirit as it has been distinctively expressed in the Charismatic Renewal. On the other hand, they are called to contribute to the diffusion of that grace throughout the whole Church, including among those who do not belong to the Charismatic Renewal. On both counts, there is need to rely on the leading of the Holy Spirit as he guides the Church through history. Relying on the Spirit requires being rooted in and dependent on the Church, recognizing that Christ confided to the Church the authority to reliably interpret the word of God and discern the work of the Spirit.

Integration of the Charismatic Renewal into the life of the Church involves both these aspects: first, growing in ecclesial maturity as a movement; and second, seeking ways to spread the culture of Pentecost throughout the whole Church and the world, especially in a rediscovery of the full power and efficacy of the sacraments of initiation.

4.1 The Catholic Charismatic Renewal as a Movement in the Church

Since 1975 the Charismatic Renewal has had a formal relationship with the hierarchy of the Church, first through Cardinal Suenens, then through Bishop (now Cardinal) Cordes and Cardinal Rylko of the Pontifical Council for the Laity, which has been a significant means of ecclesial oversight and support. Leaders in the Charismatic Renewal participate in international and local gatherings with those of other movements such as Focolare, the Neo-Catechumenal Way, Communion and Liberation, Sant'Egidio, and Schönstatt.

Some dioceses have appointed a liaison for the new ecclesial movements or formed structures for collaboration between the movements and the ordinary diocesan and parish structures.

The Charismatic Renewal is not a single entity with a unified organizational structure but rather a stream of movements and groups united by a common experience of baptism in the Spirit, including prayer groups, covenant communities, schools of evangelization, healing ministries, and a wide variety of other groups and ministries, some ecumenical and some solely Catholic. How the Renewal relates to the structures of the local church depends in part on local circumstances, but certain principles hold true everywhere. The parish constitutes the main structure in the local church for pastoral care and for the apostolate. As recent popes have pointed out, the movements serve as a kind of leaven, bringing to the local church a new fervor and missionary dynamism.[15] The parish needs the movements with their spiritual vitality, and the movements need the parish to avoid becoming closed in on themselves. The movements should cultivate a close relationship with the local bishop, who has full authority to oversee and regulate everything pertaining to faith and the apostolate in his diocese. Cardinal Ratzinger said of this relationship,

> The movements... need to be reminded that—even if they have found and transmitted the totality of the faith in their way—they are a gift to the Church as a whole, and must submit to the demands of this totality, in order to be true to their own essence. But the local churches, too, even the bishops, must be reminded that they must avoid any

uniformity of pastoral organizations and programs. They must not turn their own pastoral plans into the criterion of what the Holy Spirit is allowed to do.[16]

Cardinal Rylko has described well the spirit of mutual respect and humility that should prevail:

John Paul II never tired of insisting that the ecclesial movements and new communities are called to take their place "humbly" in dioceses and parishes, serving the Church with an attitude wholly devoid of pride or superiority with regard to other realities and with a true spirit of sincere collaboration and ecclesial communion. And at the same time the Holy Father insisted that pastors—bishops and parish priests—ought to welcome these groups "cordially," recognizing and respecting their particular charisms and accompanying them with paternal care. St. Paul's golden rule applies here: "Do not quench the Spirit. Do not despise the words of prophets, but test everything; hold fast to what is good" (1 Thes 5:19–20).[17]

At the historic gathering of lay movements at Pentecost 1998, Pope John Paul II spoke of the new movements as the "providential response of the Holy Spirit" to the critical challenges of the Church in our time. He also called the movements to grow toward "ecclesial maturity," that is, to bear the mature fruit of communion and commitment within the Church. The characteristics of ecclesial maturity, as set out in *Christifideles Laici*, 30, include giving primacy to the call to holiness, fidelity to the Church's Magisterium in doctrine and morals, communion with the pope and local bishop, sharing in the mission of the Church, and a commitment to furthering the dignity of the person in human society.

4.2 Spreading the Culture of Pentecost

Pope John Paul II addressed this exhortation to the Catholic Charismatic Renewal in 2004: "Thanks to the Charismatic Movement, a multitude of Christians, men and women, young people and adults have rediscovered Pentecost as a living reality in their daily lives. I hope that the *spirituality of Pentecost* will spread in the Church as a *renewed incentive to prayer, holiness, communion and proclamation.*"[18] On another occasion he urged leaders of the Charismatic Renewal to help bring to life the "culture of Pentecost."[19] This message has been repeated by Pope Benedict XVI.[20]

A culture is a shared way of life that embodies a society's deeply held beliefs and values. What is a culture of Pentecost? It is one where the Holy Spirit is known, loved, and frequently invoked; where the whole way of life flows from the active presence of the Spirit and his gifts. Such a culture is expressed in the liturgy and communal prayer, in family life, in music, art, education, recreation, politics, and other forms of social interaction. Characteristics of this culture would include a confident expectancy that the Lord speaks to us and acts in our lives; liturgies and prayer meetings that include joyful, spontaneous praise and worship; frequent reading and sharing from the Scriptures; close bonds of spiritual brotherhood and sisterhood, often in some form of community; an openness to God's power for healing and deliverance; an active engagement in the spiritual battle; love for God expressed in humble service to one another and to the needy; a strong impulse toward ecumenism; a zeal to bear witness to the gospel; and a longing for Christ's coming in glory. Ultimately, a culture of Pentecost—a culture of life that overthrows the culture of death—should impact and shape all of society.

The outpouring of the Spirit in the Catholic Charismatic Renewal since 1967 has already made a profound impact on the Church in many of these areas, but the Church is always in need of deeper renewal. Those who are baptized in the Spirit play an important role in calling the whole Church to return anew to the Upper Room, united in constant prayer with Mary and the disciples, expectantly awaiting a renewed coming of the Holy Spirit.

4.3 Baptism in the Spirit and the Sacraments of Initiation

The theological link between baptism in the Spirit and sacramental baptism was discussed in Part III, section 5 above. The present section offers some suggestions for pastoral application.

In the early Church, when the sacraments of initiation were most often administered to adults, it was taken for granted that Christian initiation involved a radical conversion and a transforming experience of the divine life into which the Christian was newly born. Where the sacraments are administered to infants or young children, as they normally are today, the elements of personal faith and conversion must be supplied later for the sacraments to have their full efficacy. This is especially the case where children grow up in a non-Christian or only nominally Christian environment. The Holy Spirit is given objectively through baptism and confirmation (*Catechism of the Catholic Church*, 1215, 1302), yet that gift can remain dormant in the soul. Moreover, even among adults entering the Church there is a widespread lack of understanding and expectation of the transforming power contained in the sacraments.

Thus for the renewal of the Church there is a great need to rediscover the full power and vitality of the sacraments of initiation. One way to do this is through a confirmation preparation program that would resemble a Life in the Spirit Seminar. Such a program would prepare young people, at a level appropriate to their age, to welcome the Holy Spirit into their lives with great expectancy and docility. It would include the basic proclamation of the gospel—that initial proclamation which moves a person to fall in love with Jesus and give one's whole life to him. It would teach the candidates how to rely on the power of the Holy Spirit in living as committed disciples of Christ and growing in holiness. It would also include teaching on the charisms and, after confirmation, practice in exercising them, especially in the context of evangelization. Some dioceses have already begun to implement confirmation programs of this kind. A similar approach could be developed for the Rite of Christian Initiation for Adults (RCIA).

Those who are baptized in the Spirit can play an important role in developing such programs, serving as catechists in them, and helping to ensure that the sacraments are not emptied of their power through apathy, routine, or lack of faith.

5. Pastoral Discernment

In the nearly half century since the Catholic Charismatic Renewal began, there has been tremendous growth in maturity and wisdom. Mistakes made in the early days due to ignorance and inexperience have been corrected. But as always in the Christian life, there is need for ongoing discernment, examination of conscience, and repentance so that the gifts of God do not become diluted through human error and sin.

5.1 Losing the Fire

Every new work of the Spirit faces the challenge of maintaining its initial fervor and zeal for holiness enkindled through the gift of God. There is a risk of gradually drifting away, which can sometimes occur through the temptation to overly control the work of the Spirit. Instead of a dependence on the Spirit and his gifts we can begin to rely on human plans and programs or on a particular way of doing things. Even charismatic gatherings can fall into the trap of becoming perfunctory and routine. Over time we can neglect the call to listen intently to the Lord and to speak forth his word prophetically for the sake of the Church. This can in turn lead to a loss of spiritual clarity. We can become indifferent to the spread of the gospel and the salvation of others. Jesus constantly warned his disciples of the danger of falling asleep, of becoming lukewarm, of the salt losing its flavor (Mark 13:35-37; Matt 5:13; Rev 3:16). To avoid succumbing to these dangers the Charismatic Renewal must constantly rekindle the fire of its foundational grace, the grace of Pentecost, just as did the early Christians (Acts 4:24-31; 2 Tim 1:6).

5.2 Sensationalism and False Expectations

Good discernment will help avoid sensationalism or an overemphasis on signs, wonders, resting in the Spirit, and other visible manifestations of the Spirit. While it is right to have expectant faith that God will act, it is wrong to demand specific signs of his action (see Matt 12:38-39). Likewise there can be a devaluation of the sacraments as the primary channels of grace established by Christ. Baptism in the Spirit is not a substitute for the sacraments but the source of rekindled fervor in celebrating the sacraments. There can also be an excessive focus on the demonic, which can cause unhealthy fear and hinder people from accepting responsibility for their sins. The primary focus should be on the Spirit himself as the supreme Giver and Gift of God, rather than on his particular gifts.

Similarly, some people approach baptism in the Spirit with false expectations. They may be seeking merely a spiritual high, or an immediate resolution of personal problems, or a shortcut on the path to holiness. If this is the case, when spiritual dryness or difficulties arise they quickly fall away. Baptism in the Spirit is a grace of holiness, meant to lead us to the fullness of Christian maturity. It is not an escape from the demands of discipleship: "If any man would come after me, let him deny himself and take up his cross daily and follow me" (Luke 9:23). Baptism in the Spirit *empowers* us to take up this call with divine energy. It is a grace that must continue to grow throughout a person's life as he or she yields to the Spirit on a daily basis.

5.3 Elitism and Spiritual Pride

Elitism or self-enclosed piety is a common temptation of renewal movements. Those who belong to a prayer group or community must avoid closing in on themselves with a sense of self-satisfaction. It is one thing to rejoice in and bear witness to a marvelous work of God in our lives; it is an entirely different thing to look down on others as less holy than ourselves. Likewise, we must guard against indifference to the needs of those around us, especially the pastoral needs of the local church.

The illusion that because one's prophecies or other charisms come from God they therefore need no discernment or oversight is a dangerous temptation to spiritual pride. As Scripture makes clear, every charism is subject to discernment (1 Cor 14:21; 1 Thes 5:21; 1 John 4:1). No one owns the charism he or she has been given. "No charism dispenses a person from reference and submission to the Pastors of the Church."[21]

5.4 Divisiveness

Finally, all those baptized in the Spirit, and especially leaders, must be vigilant against what has often caused great damage in the Charismatic Renewal and in the Church: divisiveness. Even in the first century, St. Paul had to admonish the Christians of Corinth for their party spirit, the "jealousy and strife" that showed that they were still "of the flesh" (1 Cor 1:10; 3:1–3). In the Charismatic Renewal, sincere differences of opinion among leaders have sometimes degenerated into bitter disagreements and the breakup of prayer groups or communities. Sowing disunity is Satan's greatest tactic for thwarting the work of God. Yet Jesus prayed on the eve of his passion "that they may all be one, even as you, Father, are in me, and I in you" (John 17:21). To the degree that each person yields to the purifying work of the Spirit, who brings forth the fruit of humility, forbearance, and love, there will be a bond of unity stronger than any dividing force. Paul's appeal holds true today:

If there is any encouragement in Christ, any incentive of love, any participation in the Spirit, any affection and sympathy, complete my joy by being of the same mind, having the same love, being in full accord and of one mind (Phil 2:1–2).

Conclusion

The gift of baptism in the Spirit and its transformation of many lives since the emergence of the Catholic Charismatic Renewal in 1967 are reason for great joy and thanksgiving to God. One can see in these developments part of the heavenly answer to the prayer that Pope John XXIII asked all Catholics to pray during the Second Vatican Council: "Lord, renew your wonders in this our day as by a new Pentecost!"

Since then, the popes have spoken in a consistent and emphatic way of the Church's need for a rekindling of Pentecostal fire. In answer to the question of what the Church needs most, Paul VI responded, "the Spirit, the Holy Spirit.... The Church needs her perennial Pentecost; she needs fire in her heart, words on her lips, prophecy in her outlook." In 1998, John Paul II exhorted nearly half a million representatives of lay movements gathered in Rome, "Today, I would like to cry out to all of you gathered here in St. Peter's Square and to all Christians: Open yourselves docilely to the gifts of the Spirit! Accept gratefully and obediently the charisms which the Spirit never ceases to bestow on us!"

Pope Benedict has continued this insistent message. In 2008 he proclaimed at World Youth Day in Australia: "Together we shall invoke the Holy Spirit, confidently asking

God for the gift of a new Pentecost for the Church and for humanity in the third millennium."[1] During his visit to the U.S. that same year, the Pope prayed: "Let us implore from God the grace of a new Pentecost for the Church in America. May tongues of fire, combining burning love of God and neighbor with zeal for the spread of Christ's Kingdom, descend on all present!"[2] At the beginning of the Special Synod for Africa, he stated that "Pentecost is not only a past event, the beginnings of the Church, but... it is today, rather, now: 'Nunc Sancte nobis Spiritus.' We pray that the Lord accomplish now the effusion of his Spirit and recreate his Church and the world."[3]

With the whole Church, those who belong to the Catholic Charismatic Renewal confidently ask the Father for a renewed outpouring of his Spirit in the third millennium and for a wide diffusion of the gift he has already given, especially to ignite the new evangelization. "Come, Holy Spirit, fill the hearts of your faithful and enkindle in them the fire of your love!"

Notes

Introduction

[1] Regina Caeli message, May 11, 2008.

[2] Ibid. In another address the pope noted that Jesus, from the moment of his own baptism, "was revealed as the One who came to baptize humanity in the Holy Spirit: he came to give men and women life in abundance (cf. Jn 10:10)." (Benedict XVI, Angelus message, January 13, 2008).

[3] In English, the term "outpouring of the Spirit" is usually used for a corporate event such as the Pentecost event described in Acts 2 or the Duquesne weekend. The term "baptism in the Spirit," in contrast, is usually used for an individual experience (see Part III, section 1).

[4] David Barrett, George Thomas Kurian, and Todd M. Johnson, *World Christian Encyclopedia: A Comparative Survey of Churches and Religions in the Modern World*, 2nd ed. (Oxford: Oxford University Press, 2001).

[5] "Historically, this 'awakening' comes to us from classical Pentecostalism, as well as from what is generally termed Neo-pentecostalism." (Cardinal Léon-Joseph Suenens, *Ecumenism and Charismatic Renewal: Theological and Pastoral Orientations*, Malines Document 2 [Ann Arbor, Mich.: Servants Books, 1978], 19; available at www.stucom.nl/algemeen/alldocnl.htm).

[6] Cardinal Walter Kasper, "Baptism in the Spirit has a fundamental role for them" (Address to College of Cardinals, 23 Nov 2007, *PCPCU Information Service*, 126 [2007/IV], pp. 187–88).

[7] See Cecil M. Robeck, Jr., *The Azusa Street Mission and Revival: The Birth of the Global Pentecostal Movement* (Nashville, TN: Thomas Nelson, 2006); Allan H. Anderson, *An Introduction to Pentecostalism: Global Charismatic Christianity* (Cambridge: Cambridge University Press, 2004).

[8] Pew Forum on Religion and Public Life, "Pentecostalism," http://pewforum.org/docs/?DocID=140.

[9] *Novo Millennio Ineunte*, 40.

[10] Benedict XVI, Letter concerning the Society of St. Pius X, March 10, 2009.

[11] *Guidelines on Prayers for Healing*, revised edition (Rome: ICCRS, 2012).

Part I: Characteristics and Fruits

[1] The term charismatic renewal (lowercase) is used here to refer to a current of grace that has been present in many Christian traditions since the Azusa Street revival of 1906, as distinct from the Catholic Charismatic Renewal as an organized movement in the Catholic Church.

[2] The affirmation of this sovereign character of God's action in baptism in the Spirit must not be understood as replacing or detracting from the essentially mediated character of God's gift of saving grace through the Church, the ordained ministry, the liturgy, and the sacraments (see Part III, section 4).

[3] Patti Gallagher Mansfield, *As by a New Pentecost* (Steubenville, OH: Franciscan University Press, 1992), 25–26.

[4] See especially *Ecclesia in America*, 8–12.

[5] See *Lumen Gentium*, especially 2–4; and *Sacrosanctum Concilium*, especially 5–6. In the *Catechism of the Catholic Church*, see the teaching on the Church as the People of God, the Body of Christ and the Temple of the Holy Spirit (781–810) and the introductory section on the liturgy and the sacraments (1077–90).

[6] Many of the songs composed within the charismatic renewal have a basic biblical inspiration, including many that are versions of psalms expressed in contemporary words and music.

[7] See *Sacrosanctum Concilium*, 7.

[8] There are other lists of charisms in the New Testament, but the Renewal has drawn special attention to those which Paul calls "spiritual gifts" in 1 Cor 12 (see Part II, section 2.3).

[9] "The charisms had disappeared not so much from the life of the Church as from her theology." (Raniero Cantalamessa, presentation at the International Colloquium on Charisms and Charismatic Renewal, Rome, April 2008; published in French as *Dons et Charismes dans la foi et la vie de l'Eglise* [Nouan-le-Fuzelier, France: Editions des Béatitudes, 2009], 68).

[10] In the Renewal there have also been numerous reports of a miraculous gift of tongues, where the speaker has spoken intelligibly in a language unknown to himself but known to a hearer. For example, Dom Louis Leloir, O.S.B., an expert in biblical languages, recounts that at a charismatic prayer meeting he was astounded to hear a young woman who knew only French addressing a prayer to the Virgin Mary in fluent ancient Syriac. Leloir, *Désert et communion*, Spiritualité Orientale, n. 26 (Bégrolles en Mauges, France: Abbaye de Bellefontaine, 1978), 230.

[11] *Lumen Gentium*, 12, in *Vatican 11: The Conciliar and Postconciliar Documents*, ed. A. Flannery (Dublin: Dominican Publications, 1975), p. 363.

[12] This topic is treated in more detail in the document *Guidelines on Prayers for Healing*, revised edition (Rome: ICCRS, 2012).

[13] See Matt 8:16; 10:8; Mark 1:34; 6:13; 16:17–18; Acts 5:16; 8:7; 10:38; 19:12. The subject was directly addressed in the paper of Rufus Pereira at the International Colloquium on Prayer for Healing held in Rome in 2001, "Exorcism and Deliverance for Healing, Reconciliation, and New Life," in *Prayer for Healing* (Rome: ICCRS, 2003), 237-251.

[14] The pastoral issues raised by these ministries were treated in *Guidelines on Prayers for Healing*, and are addressed briefly in Part IV below.

[15] Raniero Cantalamessa notes that many revival movements of the past "ended in schism and developed into sects instead of renewing the Church," but that "This has not happened with the Catholic Charismatic Renewal, and we ought to give credit for this, even more to the courage of popes like Paul VI, John Paul II and Benedict XVI than to the members of the Renewal." Cantalamessa, presentation at the International Colloquium on Baptism in the Holy Spirit, Rome, March 17-20, 2011.

[16] See Paul Josef Cordes, *Call to Holiness: Reflections on the Catholic Charismatic Renewal* (Collegeville, Minn.: Liturgical Press, 1997), 38.

[17] *Evangelii Nuntiandi*, 75.

[18] "The Renewal in the Spirit, as we behold it today, is manifesting itself as a substantially similar event in most of the Christian Churches and denominations." (Léon-Joseph Suenens, *Ecumenism and Charismatic Renewal*, 21).

[19] "When Christians pray together, the goal of unity seems closer." (*Ut Unum Sint*, 22).

[20] *Ecumenism and Charismatic Renewal*, 19.

Part II: Biblical and Patristic Foundations

[1] Cf. John 16:14-15; Rom 8:26. The Hebrew term for God's Spirit, *ruach*, can mean spirit, wind, or breath. In the Old Testament, the Spirit of God refers to the divine breath that makes inert flesh into living human beings (Ps 104:30; cf. Ezek 37:10, 14) and that empowers people to do exceptional deeds (Exod 31:3; Judg 14:6).

[2] See, for instance, Gen 4:1; Isa 47:8; Jer 16:21; Hos 6:3.

[3] This passage can also be punctuated differently to read, "If anyone is thirsty, let him come to me and drink. Whoever believes in me, as the scripture has said, 'Out of his heart shall flow rivers of living water.'" In this case the *believer* becomes a spring from which flows the life-giving water of the Spirit; in the other case *Jesus* is the spring. Both interpretations are legitimate.

[4] Note the parallel with the coming of the Spirit on Jesus at his own baptism, when he was at prayer (Luke 3:21-22).

[5] Acts 1:8 serves as a kind of table of contents: after the Spirit is poured out in Acts 2, the gospel is proclaimed "in Jerusalem" in Acts 2-7, "in Judea and Samaria" in Acts 8-12, and "to the ends of the earth," i.e., as far as Rome, in Acts 13-28.

[6] See also the theophany to Elijah at Mount Horeb (Sinai) in 1 Kings 19:11-13.

[7] Acts 6:56; 9:10-16; 10:3-6, 9-20; 16:9; 18:9; 22:17-21; 23:11.

[8] Note that Luke uses a wealth of terminology to designate the Spirit's coming: people are "baptized in the Holy Spirit" (Acts 1:5; 11:16) or "filled with the Holy Spirit" (2:4; 9:17; 4:31); they "receive the Holy Spirit" (2:38; 8:15-19; 10:47; 19:2); the Spirit is "poured out" (2:17-18, 33; 10:45); the Spirit "falls on" (8:16; 10:44; 11:15) or "comes on" people (1:8; 19:6); God "gives" the Spirit (5:32; 8:18; 11:17; 15:8).

[9] Acts 2:47; 3:8; 4:21; 5:41; 11:18, 23; 13:48, 52; 15:3; 16:23-25; 21:19-20.

[10] Acts 2:4, 11; 10:44-46; 11:27-28; 19:6; 21:9-11; 15:32-33; 13:1-3.

[11] Acts 4:13, 31; 5:18-25, 40; 7:60; 8:3; 12:1-3; 16:23; 20:22-23; 28:31.

[12] Luke does not explain why this second step is needed, but one possibility is that Philip's mission in Samaria was a new step for the early Church, which had to be officially confirmed by the apostles. Luke does not indicate that only apostles can pray for others to receive the Spirit. In Acts 9:17, Paul receives the Spirit at the hands of Ananias, who is simply described as a "disciple."

[13] See the *Catechism*, 1315.

[14] James D. G. Dunn, *Jesus and the Spirit*, 2nd ed. (Grand Rapids: Eerdmans, 1997), 226.

[15] Faith and hope in their present form will pass away in eternity, for "who hopes for what he sees?" (Rom 8:24; see 2 Cor 4:18; 5:7), but in this life they are, with love, the foundation on which the edifice of the Church is built.

[16] George Montague, *The Holy Spirit: Growth of a Biblical Tradition* (New York: Paulist: 1976), 155.

[17] The most thorough treatment of baptism in the Spirit in the early Church is the study by Kilian McDonnell and George T. Montague, *Christian Initiation and Baptism in the Spirit: Evidence from the First Eight Centuries*, 2nd ed. (Collegeville, Minn.: Liturgical Press, 1994). See also the response of Norbert Baumert, *Charisma–Taufe–Geisttaufe* (Würzburg: Echter, 2001).

[18] St. Cyril of Jerusalem, *Catechetical Lectures*, 17.19, quoted in Raniero Cantalamessa, *Sober Intoxication of the Spirit*, trans. Marsha Daigle-Williamson (Cincinnati: Servant, 2005), 2-3.

[19] Quoted in Cantalamessa, *Sober Intoxication of the Spirit*, 1.

[20] *Sermon* 267.3. See also Augustine, *Sermon* 225.

[21] St. Justin Martyr, *Dialogue with Trypho*, 29.1; Origen, *On Jeremiah*, 2.3; Didymus the Blind, *On the Trinity*, 2.12; St. Cyril of Jerusalem, *Catechetical Lectures*, 17.18.

[22] *Proto-Catechesis*, 12.

[23] *On Matthew*, 2:6. See also *Catechetical Lectures*, 3.1, 3; Diodochus of Photike, *A Hundred Chapters*, LXXVII (Sources Chrétiennes 5 bis), 135.

[24] *Treatise to Donatus on the Grace of God*, paraphrased by Anne Field in *From Darkness to Light. What It Meant to Become a Christian in the Early Church* (Ann Arbor: Servant, 1978), 190–92.

[25] *Dialogue with Trypho*.

[26] *Against Heresies*, 5.6.1.

[27] *Against Heresies*, 2.32.4.

[28] *On Baptism*, 20.

[29] *Catechetical Lectures*, 17.19; 18.32; cf. 17.37.

[30] *On the Trinity*, 2.35.

[31] *Tract on the Psalms*, 64.14–15.

[32] For further hypoteses on why the decline occurred, see McDonnell and Montague, *Christian Initiation*, 116–132.

[33] *Retractions*, I.13.7.

[34] *The City of God*, XXII.8.

[35] *City of God*, XXII.8.

[36] *Sermon* 38.2.

[37] *Second Apology* 6.5–6.

[38] The Fathers did not refer to jubilation as "speaking in tongues" (*glossolalia*), probably because they associated tongues with the Pentecost phenomenon of Acts 2, where the tongues were heard as actual human languages rather than non-conceptual speech.

[39] *On the Psalms*, 99.3.

[40] *On the Psalms*, 97.4.

[41] *Moralia*, 8.89; cf. 24.10; 28.35. See also Pseudo-Jerome, *Breviarium in Psalmos*, XXVI; Cassiodorus, Ps 32.3; 80.1; 97.5; Isidore of Seville, *Opera Omnia*, V.43

⁴² See Tertullian, *Apology*, 39; Egeria, *The Diary of a Pilgrimage*, trans. George E. Gingres (Paramus, NJ: Newman Press, 1970), 92; F. Van Der Meer, *Augustine the Bishop* (New York: Sheed and Ward, 1961), 339.

⁴³ Medieval mystics such as Richard Rolle (1300–1349) write of jubilation: "In the depths of his being there is the praise of God and jubilant song, and his praise bursts out aloud"; God "would reveal to me the song I long to understand, and he would make plain and clear my joyous shout." Rolle, *The Fire of Love*, 32–34, trans. Clifton Wolters (Harmondsworth, U.K. / Baltimore: Penguin Books, 1972), 146, 153. See also St. Teresa of Avila, *Interior Castle*, VI.6.10–11.

Part III: Theological Reflection

¹ Ann Arbor, Mich.: Word of Life, 1974. Available at www.stucom.nl/algemeen/alldocnl.htm.

² "Effusion" is a rare word in English and is usually not used in relation to the Holy Spirit. "Outpouring" (like the German term "Erweckung," awakening) usually refers to a corporate event touching many people rather than an individual experience.

³ Angelus message on the feast of the Baptism of the Lord, January 13, 2008.

⁴ This new awareness of the Spirit's work of sanctification calls for a rediscovery of the immense spiritual resources of the Catholic tradition, both from the patristic period and from the lives of the great saints and spiritual masters—resources that are urgently needed for the new evangelization. See John Paul II, *Novo Millennio Ineunte*, 33.

⁵ The International Colloquium on Charisms and Charismatic Renewal, held in Rome in 2008, represents an important step forward in meeting this need, as does the earlier International Colloquium on Prayer for Healing (2001). But the contributions and discussions demonstrated the newness of this topic. In particular, some of the renewal leaders testified to having to develop their own understanding and practice in an area for which their formation had not prepared them.

⁶ See, for instance, St. Augustine, *Tractates in the Gospel of John*, LIV.12.8: God "has awakened in us a great longing for that sweet

experience of his presence within; it is by daily growth that we acquire it"; and St. Bernard, *Sermons on the Song of Songs* 1.11: "Let those without experience burn with desire so that they will not so much know as experience."

[7] John Paul II, address at the World Congress of Ecclesial Movements, May 27, 1998. Italics in the original.

[8] John Paul II, address to members of Ecclesial Movements and New Communities, May 30, 1998.

[9] In classical terminology charisms are referred to as *gratiae gratis datae* (graces freely given) in distinction from the *gratia gratum faciens* (sanctifying grace) imparted through the sacraments. This distinction from the Church's tradition is important for the present-day elaboration of the relationship between the institutional and the charismatic. St. Thomas Aquinas treats charisms extensively in his *Summa Theologiae*, II-II, 171–178.

[10] See Cardinal Joseph Ratzinger, "The Ecclesial Movements: A Theological Reflection on Their Place in the Church," in *Movements in the Church. Proceedings of the World Congress of the Ecclesial Movements* (Vatican City: Pontificium Consilium pro Laicis, 1999), 23-51. Available at www.stucom.nl/algemeen/alldocnl.htm.

[11] For an ecumenical perspective on this question, see *On Becoming a Christian: Insights from Scripture and the Patristic Writings With Some Contemporary Reflections*, Report of the Fifth Phase of the International Dialogue Between Some Classical Pentecostal Churches and Leaders and the Catholic Church (1998-2006), par. 227-234, published in PCPCU Information Service 129 (2008/III), pp. 206-7. Available at www.stucom.nl/algemeen/alldocnl.htm.

[12] See the *Catechism*, 1216, 1265-66, 1302-03.

[13] It is important to note that baptism of infants is a priceless gift and an immemorial tradition of the Church (*Catechism*, 1250-52). In itself, however, it is not sufficient for the flowering of baptismal grace (*Catechism*, 1231).

[14] In classical terminology, a sacrament is given validly *ex opere operato* (by very fact of the action being performed); but the actual fruitfulness of the sacrament in a person's life is *ex opere operantis* (from the action of the doer), that is, it is dependent on subjective factors such as the quality of

the preparation, the effectiveness of the minister, and especially the faith of the recipient.

[15] See Augustine, *Sermo* 269.2; Thomas Aquinas, *Summa Theologiae*, III, 67–71, especially 69.8.

[16] *Summa Theologiae* I, 43, 6 ad 2.

[17] Apostolic exhortation *Christifideles Laici* (1988), 31. See also the third criterion for authentic "Ecclesiality" on "The Witness to a strong and authentic communion" outlined in *Christifideles Laici* 30.

[18] See Matt 10:7–8; Luke 9:2; 10:9; Mark 16:15–18; 1 Cor 14:1.

[19] As St. Augustine wrote, "The Spirit is promised not only to him who does not have, but also to him who already has. For it is given to one who has not, in order that he may have; and to one who has, that he may have more abundantly" (*Tractates on the Gospel of John*, 74.2).

Part IV: Pastoral Issues

[1] *Catechesi Tradendae*, 19.

[2] Address in Bogota, Colombia, March 9, 2006, available at http://catholiconline.com/featured/headline.php?ID=3166.

[3] A variety of titles are used for the course, such as Holy Spirit Seminar, New Life Seminar, Born in the Spirit Seminar, and so on.

[4] See Raniero Cantalamessa, *Sober Intoxication of the Spirit*, 40–41.

[5] See the *Séminaire de Vie dans l'Esprit* used in Benin, Africa, supplied by Jean Pliya.

[6] On the sanctifying gifts of the Spirit, see the *Catechism*, 1831; on the charismatic gifts see 798–801.

[7] John Paul II, *Christifideles Laici*, 28.

[8] Paul VI, *Evangelii Nuntiandi*, 5; John Paul II, *Redemptoris Missio*, 3.

[9] Paul Josef Cordes, *Call to Holiness*, 13.

[10] Ibid., 14.

[11] Ibid., 13. See, for instance, Gen 48:14; Deut 34:9; 2 Kg 13:16; Mark 10:16; Luke 4:40; Acts 9:17; 13:3.

[12] See McDonnell and Montague, *Christian Initiation*, 89.

[13] It is important to recognize that prophetic words do not give new revelation adding to the deposit of faith, but make the unchanging revelation of Christ come alive in a new way for the present generation.

[14] Cardinal Suenens wrote in 1986, "as long as we envisage the charismatic Renewal as just one of several spiritual 'movements', we are losing sight of its specific grace, which is permeating the Church. In fact, it is not a movement in the usual sociological sense of the term.... It can best be described as a 'current of grace'... a movement or breath of the Holy Spirit, valid for every Christian" (*Resting in the Spirit: Malines Document 6* [Dublin: Veritas, 1986], 2; available at www.stucom.nl/algemeen/alldocnl.htm).

[15] See John Paul II, Address of May 30, 1998; and Cardinal Ratzinger in *The Ratzinger Report. An Exclusive Interview on the State of the Church* (San Francisco: Ignatius, 1985), 43–44.

[16] Ratzinger, "Ecclesial Movements," 50.

[17] Rylko, Address in Bogotá, Colombia, March 9, 2006.

[18] Vespers homily, May 29, 2004. For a compilation of papal messages to the Catholic Charismatic Renewal, see *"Then Peter stood up..." Collection of the Popes' addresses to the CCR from its origin to the year 2000* (Rome: ICCRS, 2000). Many national bishops' conferences have also issued positive statements on the Renewal; the earliest of these were collected in a three-volume work by Kilian McDonnell, *Presence, Power, Praise: Documents on the Charismatic Renewal* (Collegeville, Minn.: Liturgical Press, 1980).

[19] Audience with members of the National Service Committee and of the Council of the Italian association Rinnovamento nello Spirito, March 14, 2002.

[20] Benedict XVI, general audience of Sept. 28, 2005.

[21] *Christifideles Laici*, 24.

Conclusion

[1] Benedict XVI, XXIII World Youth Day, Sydney, Australia, July 23, 2008.

[2] Benedict XVI, Homily at St. Patrick's Cathedral, New York, April 19, 2008.

Notes

[3] Benedict XVI, Address given at the opening of the First General Congregation of the Second Special Assembly for Africa of the Synod of Bishops, October 5, 2009.